TEAMWORK: WORKING TOGETHER IN THE HUMAN SERVICES

TEAMWORK: WORKING TOGETHER IN THE HUMAN SERVICES

NAOMI ISGRIG BRILL
University of Nebraska

J. B. Lippincott Company

Philadelphia

New York / San Jose / Toronto

Copyright © 1976 by J. B. Lippincott Company
All rights reserved.

With the exception of brief excerpts for review, no
part of this book may be reproduced in any form or by
any means without written permission from the publisher.

ISBN 0–397–47342–7 (cloth)
     0–397–47343–5 (paper)
Library of Congress Catalog Card Number 75–45229

Printed in the United States of America

 3 5 7 9 8 6 4 2

Library of Congress Cataloging in Publication Data

Brill, Naomi I
    Teamwork: working together in the human services.

    Includes bibliographies and index.
    1. Social service—Team work. I. Title.
HV41.B66   361   75–45229
ISBN 0–397–47342–7
ISBN 0–397–47343–5 pbk.

This book is dedicated to colleagues, teachers, and practitioners in human service, who gave me the greatest gifts of all—time and the freedom to work; who answered my questions patiently; who loaned me their books, shared their ideas, and provided emotional support and sustenance . . .

. . . to the indispensable clerical workers, without whom it would be impossible to function . . .

. . . with the hope that each reader will find something here that will be useful.

American society is undergoing a total replacement of its philosophical concepts. Words are being emptied of old meanings and new values are coming in to fill the vacuum. Racial antagonisms, inflation, ecological destruction, and power groups are all symptoms of the emergence of a new world view of man and his society. Today thought patterns are shifting from the traditional emphasis on the solitary individual to as yet unrelated definitions of man as a member of a specific group. (Vine Deloria, Jr., *We Talk, You Listen*, New York: Delta, 1970)

The real conflict we face now is a conflict not between the old and the new, but between the new and the futuristic, between what is known and what is emerging, between the individual and the new emerging image of what might be termed the collectivised individual. The whole person is not and cannot be totally individual; part of the whole, today more than ever, must be nonindividualized, communal or collectivised. For we all live in a social environment with others. And that social environment, explosive with change, by continually impinging on us, becomes part of us. (Irving H. Buchan, "Humanism and Futurism: Enemies or Allies?" from *Learning for Tomorrow*, Alvin Toeffler, ed., New York: Random House, 1974)

CONTENTS

1 The Human Services in the Seventies 1

Social systems reflect the society which gives birth to them, and the current major social changes are reflected in the institutions designed for the provision of human service. This chapter surveys these changing trends, which set the stage for changes in education and in practice.

2 The Evolving Team Concept 15

One result of changing social demands, knowledge resources, and program development has been the increasingly widespread use of team models of practice. The concept of teaming is being studied both as to theoretical base and practical application. This chapter deals with the factors related to its development and with the meaning and use of consultation, collaboration, and referral.

3 The Individual as a Team Member 29

Individuals are first, last, and always unique persons, and this uniqueness must be considered in development and use of teams. This chapter is an analysis of the complementary duality of personal/worker characteristics that affect the individual's ability to be a useful team member.

4 The Internal Life of the Team, I 45

Teams can be conceptualized as dynamic units which are characterized by a developmental pattern that can be understood and controlled. This chapter proposes a model for understanding the factors involved in team formation, structure, and composition.

5 The Internal Life of the Team, II 62

The evolving team must reach an accommodation on individual value differences and develop a value system and behavioral norms of its own. On the basis of these, patterns for implementing three fundamental processes communication, conflict resolution, and decision-making must be developed.

6 The Internal Life of the Team, III 83

Teams are composed of sets of roles which complement each other. Modern teams strive toward flexibility in role definition, which makes for a volatile climate within the team. This chapter considers the factors that operate in defining roles, the significance of power, and the meaning of position and status to the team's functioning.

7 The External Life of the Team 103

Teams can be viewed as systems involved in a complex set of interrelationships with their environment. This chapter considers the team as a subsystem of larger systems and surveys the factors involved in construction and use of linkages between them.

8 The Working Team 121

The problem-solving team in human services utilizes a dynamic self-renewing process. This chapter proposes a model for understanding and knowingly using such a process.

9 Education for Teamwork 134

The team member, in both aspects of his person/ worker dyad, needs specific preparation for teamwork. This chapter discusses the factors important in designing and implementing such educational programs and suggests various content that should be included.

Appendix A: Invitation to Introspection 146

Appendix B: A Functional Yardstick for Team Analysis 149

Index 153

pREfACE

The philosopher Santayana is credited with the comment that those who do not know history are doomed to repeat history. This can be paraphrased with regard to research, and nowhere is it more applicable than to research in human service, where the ultimate goal is putting what has been learned into practice in that most difficult and demanding of arenas—work with people.

In a compilation on utilization of research principles in mental health, the National Institute of Mental Health quotes Glaser and Marx as saying in 1966:

> All over the world people struggle with problems and seek solutions. Often those who struggle are unaware that others face similar problems, and, in some instances, are solving them. It is destructive and wasteful that people should be frustrated and often defeated by difficulties for which somebody else has found a remedy.... The gap between what we know and what we put to effective use bedevils many fields of human activity—science, teaching, business management and organizations which provide health and welfare services.*

*National Institute of Mental Health, *A Distillation of Principles on Research Utilization*, Vol. I, DHEW publ. no. (HSM) 71-9060 (Washington, D.C.: U.S. Government Printing Office, 1971), p. 3.

In general in human services, practitioners tend to rely on their intuition, their prior experience and education, and their common sense in working with human problems. When faced with situations where these resources prove inadequate, they tend to consult supervisors and colleagues rather than turn to the literature, and the result is often a compounding of ignorance. Practitioners also often experience difficulty in understanding the language of researchers and in having ready access to the results of really significant studies. Caught as they are in the day-to-day emergencies and demand of human need, the pressure to produce answers frequently results in applying findings of studies beyond their validity, and in ensuing disillusionment, practitioners tend to turn their backs on ideas for changed ways of working that grow out of research findings and adhere dogmatically to old ways.

Researchers, on the other hand, also contribute to the gap between knowledge and practice. Not only is there a time lag in publication of the results of studies, there is a basic problem in communication. Researchers tend to write for other researchers and to think and behave differently from practitioners, and all too often, they are data-bound, incapable of exercising the process of adaptation of their knowledge to practice, which calls for elements of what, for lack of a better term, we call artistry.

As always, this is not a matter of absolutes. In spite of the continuing scorn of some academicians for application of theoretical knowledge and for practice as callings of lesser status, more and more "knowledge builders" are becoming "knowledge appliers," particularly in the area of human behavior, to the extent that Jimmy Durante's comment, "Everybody wants to get into the act," seems almost applicable. Perhaps out of the increasing involvement of researchers and theoreticians in practice situations and out of practitioners' increasing their commitment to ongoing education and to examining what they are thinking and doing in light of tested knowledge will come a bridge for this gap.

Teamwork is an effort to help in constructing this bridge. Its aim is to facilitate the translation of the empirical knowledge we possess about being a part of and working in groups into a form that can be applied by human service practitioners who are team members.

Naomi Isgrig Brill
September 1975

iNTRODUCTION

Group membership begins at birth and extends inevitably throughout the total life experience. In spite of this, we tend, for a variety of reasons, to be less than effective in much of our work with other people. For the past half century, efforts have been made to study group life, to understand what is involved and to be able to anticipate outcomes of particular patterns of operating so that such experiences can be consciously planned and used to achieve desired ends. Gradually, we are developing a body of tested knowledge that can be applied to specific situations and evaluated for results.

The specific situation in this instance is use of the team model in delivery of human service. The recent proliferation and resulting necessary specialization of knowledge regarding the human condition has made adoption and use of this model inevitable. Increasingly, it is found not only in health care, which has used it for many years, but also in most other areas of human service and in a wide variety of forms and settings.

Introduction

Under the aegis of teamwork, strange bedfellows are discovering, in time, that they must *learn* to work together before they *can* work together.

This book represents, then, an effort to acquaint present and future team members with the knowledge that we have painstakingly garnered about group membership and team operation in the hope that it will enable them to perform more effectively. It can only be considered a very small beginning but one which, perhaps, will help the reader develop motivation to seek additional theoretical and experiential learning. This is doubly essential, because teaming is a dynamic concept in the process of development and change. Mastery of existent knowledge serves not only as a prescription for present action but also enables us to begin to perceive and define the fundamental questions that must be answered if teamwork is to remain a vital entity.

Before we begin, we should define the major terms on which this book is based, teamwork and human service.

> *Teamwork is that work which is done by a group of people who possess individual expertise, who are responsible for making individual decisions, who hold a common purpose, and who meet together to communicate, share, and consolidate knowledge, from which plans are made, future decisions are influenced, and actions are determined.*

This is a comprehensive definition, broadly applicable to teams in all settings. The term "human service," as used here, has a similar broad application.

> *Human service designates those systems which have been developed to serve the needs of the individual and his society, to provide the essentials that will lead to realization of his maximum potential for growth and development, and to prevent or relieve his sufferings.*

The text of the book will expand these definitions.

At the end of each chapter, there is a brief list of related readings that will serve as a starting point in the student's search for additional knowledge about particular topics. Each of these, in turn, contains its own bibliography. Sources of information and ideas will, like interest on any good investment, compound once a beginning has been made. For the student or teacher whose familiarity with the whole area of groupwork and teamwork is limited, several excellent references that may be used for supplementary reading are listed at the end of this introduction.

Finally, a word of encouragement. Teamwork is not an easy process to understand or practice. It is not hard to get lost in the great number of variables that impinge upon it. This is equally true of all human relationships, however, and as always with such relationships, the rewards for risk can be great. There are many things we have yet to learn about how to work most effectively in teams, but what we do know is that teams are worth trying, and we can only go on from there.

Related Readings

Brieland, Donald; Briggs, Thomas and Luenberger, Paul: The Team Model in Social Work Practice. Syracuse, N.Y.: Syracuse University School of Social Work, 1973.
Excellent, usable monograph on various aspects of teamwork in social work practice; unusually good survey of the literature.
Horowitz, John J.: Team Practice and the Specialist. Springfield, Ill.: Charles C. Thomas, 1970.
A book of questions rather than answers, but very provocative of different ideas.
Klein, Alan F.: Social Work Through Group Practice. Albany: State University of New York at Albany, 1970.
Effective Groupwork. New York: Association Press, 1972.
Well-written, with numerous examples to illustrate points; particular emphasis placed on the importance of values and the philosophical basis for work.
Miles, Matthew B.: Learning to Work in Groups. New York: Teachers' College Press, 1959.
One of the ageless books, practical and extremely useful in its organization and presentation.
Schein, E.H.; Process Consultation. Reading, Mass.: Addison-Wesley, 1969.
Fundamentals presented from another point of view, which opens a new dimension in thinking about practice.
Wise, Harold; Beckhard, Richard; Rubin, Irwin and Kyte, Aileen: Making Health Teams Work. Cambridge, Mass.: Ballinger, 1974.
A modern application of what we know of team practice in a difficult setting; well-written, good illustrations of principles, and crammed with ideas that are universally applicable.

CHAPTER 1

The Human services
in The seventies

According to anthropologists, primitive humans
managed to survive the grinding cold and desola-
tion of the Great Ice Age in the Pleistocene era by
huddling in caves in the Pyrenees mountains. We
cannot know exactly what sort of social system
people had at that time, but we do know from
the study of artifacts that it was a communal
system and that it provided protection and nur-
ture for the young, who have the longest period
of dependency of any life form. In terms of the
demands of the era and the developmental stage
of the species, the relationship between the individual and the group and the definition of the
rights and responsibilities of each were spelled
out and, in some manner, enforced. The bison
and antelope pictured on the walls of these caves
probably could not have been killed by a lone
hunter: the differential skill of the person who
could make stone tools was essential; the warmth
of many bodies probably made the difference of
death or life during those long, cold nights. It was
a reciprocal arrangement. The group could survive

1

only if the individual members were strong, healthy, and capable of contributing to the whole; the individual could survive only with the group's protection and strength.

During the million year stretch of Pleistocene time, marked evolutionary changes took place in humanity; people came forth from the caves with brains greatly increased in size and utility, as evidenced by the artifacts of the era. Building with these tools, humankind built up to the tremendously complex society of the twentieth century; and yet, the major unsolved problem, the never-completed task, the critical dilemma is still that of defining the relationship between the individual and the society, between the group and the whole of society. The basic formula remains the same; in terms of the demands of the times and the developmental stage of the species, mutual rights and responsibilities must be spelled out and enforced. A balance must be achieved between the needs of the individual and those of the society, if both are to be healthy and strong.

Evolution of a Service-oriented Society

In our complicated modern society, social institutions are developed and charged with meeting individual needs that in a simpler time were the responsibility of the family or small group. Provision of the basic necessities of life—of what have become known as the "human services"—is vested in such institutions, as they occupy an increasingly larger and more significant part of the total social system. These social institutions reflect the climate of the society and change with changing social conditions and demands.

The Expanding and Changing Population

At present, American society is undergoing certain major changes that are markedly affecting the character of its human service institutions. Not only has there been a rapid expansion of the total population, with a resultant increasing demand for services due to the sheer numbers of people involved, there has also been, within that population growth, a disproportionate increase of those more vulnerable groups of people whose need for specialized and extensive services is greatest. Three groups constitute an increasingly larger proportion of the total United States population: the young, the aged, and the minority groups.

People under twenty-five are in the process of growing and learning to live and thus require extensive service from a society committed to promoting maximum human development, both as a moral
responsibility and as a way of ensuring its own survival and effective
functioning. Probably at no stage in life are the needs for specialized
services greater than during the formative years. For its next genera-
tion, the society must ensure provision of the basic necessities of
life, food, clothing, and shelter; must provide education and opportunities for healthy socialization; must furnish an environment
conducive to physical, emotional, and spiritual well-being; and, at
the same time, supply care for those whose needs in these areas are
in excess of the normal maturational ones, the sick, the handicapped,
the delinquent.

The aged are, by definition, people over sixty-five, although there
is some indication that this arbitrary cutoff point will be revised upward because of our increasing knowledge of the aging process. The
aged as a group are growing both numerically and proportionately;
and they also comprise a group for whom extensive services from the
society are essential. In part, this is caused by a compulsory retire-
ment system that frequently involves not only loss of income but
also psychological problems, which exacerbate that trend of increasing dependency which is a normal part of this life stage. The
great need is not only to maintain life (to which society is committed) in this group especially vulnerable to the great social diseases
of the times, cancer, emphysema, arthritis and rheumatism, and
pulmonary failure, but also to maintain *meaningful* life for these
people in a society that indicates constantly in many subtle and some
not-so-subtle ways that being old is being a burden. It is interesting
that at this time, when the trend is toward integration of all other
groups into the social picture to a greater extent, the aged are being
segregated in special communities, housing developments, and institutions, where they can be forgotten except on holidays, just as
the insane, the delinquent, the retarded, and the ill were treated
100 years ago.

Finally, the number of people in minority groups, from whom
the benefits of the social system have traditionally been withheld, is
growing: the American Indians, the blacks, the Mexican Americans,
the Asiatic Americans, women, and the poor. The intensifying
problems of these groups constitute a graphic example of what
happens in a society which does not take care of its own members,
which does not ensure social justice for all, and which tends to

perpetuate an economic system based on exploitation of the many for the benefit of the few. Among these groups, the normal needs for human services are exacerbated by the results of up to 200 years of neglect and/or second-rate services, and, as a result, the problems are more severe and the demands greater.

Changing Values

In addition to the expanding size and changing composition of population, the very nature of the social system, itself, in its increasing complexity, places additional demands on its members to achieve adequate social functioning and thus creates even greater need for human services. Perhaps, in time, the easier, fuller, more simplified life that science and technology promise will be within man's grasp, but for the present, we find ourselves all too often lost in a tangle of interlocking systems, "playing wet nurse to computers that are not yet housebroken," and striving to cope with a society so complicated that we can find no handhold from which to begin to function or make changes. At the moment, living well and fully requires a kind of sophisticated knowledge, skill, and dogged endurance that is beyond the grasp of many people.

Along with these concrete, easily documented social changes has come a subtler change, one that has affected the balance between the individual and his society—the changing value system. Values serve a dual role for people. They spell out those things that are important and worth striving for and thereby define not only goals but the manner in which these goals are to be reached. They also constitute a source for much of the personal motivation to realize these goals. Basically, this country was founded on the belief that every individual was worthwhile, that each was entitled to the good life, and that all could and should attain it. But the converse of this, that there is something morally wrong with the person who fails to fulfill himself and that he thus deserves his problems, was very much a part of pioneer life in the New World. The highest attainment was to pull oneself up by ones' bootstraps, and the news and literature of the era abounded with such successes.

This belief of self-determination persisted through the Industrial Revolution and the first quarter of the twentieth century, but with the advent of the Great Depression, the drought and the dust storms, more and more people realized that there are forces in life that individuals cannot control, as well as circumstances that make it impossible for a person to live well. With this realization came the growing conviction that, while the individual does have a right to the good life, it is the responsibility of society to provide the resources by which it may be attained. This value derives in part from moral and ethical grounds in both the Judeo-Christian doctrine and the philosophical bases of democracy, but as is so often true with moral precepts, it is frequently a value which attracts more lip service than actual acceptance. There is also marked difference of opinion about how this value should be operationalized, but, in general, there is increasing acceptance of it as a legitimate and necessary social responsibility. Historically, for example, we have moved from the concept that universal primary and secondary education should be provided for all to extension of this responsibility to include the more advanced, continuous learning necessary for living in a volatile, sophisticated society. Likewise, the principle of universal health care provided from tax funds is no longer questioned; debate has now evolved to consideration of the best plan for providing it. And public housing and legal services for those unable to afford them, even a guaranteed annual income, are either being implemented or in the process of discussion prior to implementation.

The nature of the political process creates ups and downs in commitment of resources to these programs, but the general trend is toward acceptance of both the underlying value system and the subsequent increases in the cost to society of provision of such services, in the numbers of people involved in providing the services, and in the numbers of people receiving the services. (See Table 1.)

The Knowledge Explosion

The changing size and composition of the population and the changing values relating to the nature and definition of the relationship between individuals and society are complemented by yet a third major development, the so-called "knowledge explosion" and the acceptance and use of it as a basis for action. Ever since people decided they did not necessarily have to suffer here on earth in order to receive reward in heaven and discovered that humanity is not the center of the universe, people began to examine themselves, to try to learn what kind of creature Homo sapiens really is. This search for self-knowledge received a tremendous boost in the nine-

TABLE 1 Public and Private Expenditures for Social Welfare Purposes, Fiscal 1974

	Income Maintenance		Health		Education		Welfare and Other Services		Total	
	$	%	$	%	$	%	$	%	$	%
Public	107,035	85.4	41,311	39.6	72,925	83.9	17,465	86.2	242,396[a]	71.1
Private	18,350	14.6	62,929	60.4	14,600	16.1	2,800	13.8	98,679	28.9
TOTAL	125,385	100.0	104,240[c]	100.0	87,525	100.0	20,265	100.0	341,075[b]	100.0

[a]Represents 18% of GNP. Twenty-five years ago, the comparable figure was about 10%. Represents about 56% of all government expenditures, federal, state, and local.
[b]Represents almost 25% of GNP, including private expenditures. Twenty-five years ago, the comparable figure was about 16%.
[c]Represents 7.7% of the GNP. It is estimated that an adequate universal coverage health insurance program would cost approximately 12% of the GNP.

Source: Adapted from Social Security Bulletin, January 1975, in millions of dollars (add six zeros). (These figures contain an error, but the trend they indicate is valid.)

teenth century, which was marked by "thinking giants" like Freud and Darwin, and has continued into the twentieth century, with the inescapable realizations that the really crucial problems lie in the area of humanity's inability to deal with itself and that hard knowledge is essential to decisions and actions in this area. Accordingly, there is currently great investment in time, money, and manpower devoted to knowledge-building and knowledge applications, and the results, good, bad, and indifferent, are so voluminous, they are almost overwhelming.

These three social developments—the clearly demonstrated need, the underlying basic value change, the accumulation and use of knowledge—are reflected in legislation and provision of funds, both public and private, to implement programs of education and research, prevention and remediation of human problems, and maximization of human potential. According to contemporary thinkers like Daniel Bell, the political response is a signal of change in the very nature of the society:

> ...[from] a goods producing to a service economy. Dramatic increases in the number and proportion of the work force engaged in services—and particularly in that category of services dealing with health, education, research and government—is taking place.*

Development of Social Service Systems

Social systems reflect the society that gives birth to them, and the three fundamental changes outlined above are the source of pressures for internal changes to take place within the human service systems, to an extent beyond the normal pattern of growth and change that characterizes vital systems. We can summarize the major system responses under seven specific headings:

1. The increasing size, scope, bureaucratization, and dehumanization of the human service systems.
2. The impact of scientific knowledge and technology.
3. The push for "accountability."
4. Emergence of the consumer as a participant in service planning and delivery.

*Daniel Bell, *The Coming of Post Industrial Society* (New York: Basic Books, 1973), p. 15.

   5. The politicization of the systems.
   6. The changing meaning and use of the community.
   7. The use of teams in all parts of the systems.

As always, there are both assets and liabilities inherent in each of these developments, and they can be considered only briefly for purposes of clarity in perception. In reality, all affect and are affected by each other and are inseparable parts of the total.

Size and Complexity

Society's triple mandate to its human service systems—to remedy breakdown, to prevent future breakdown, and to identify needs and provide resources for maximization of potential for human development—obviously involves a wide scope of operation. With increasing awareness of the interrelatedness of human problems has come the realization that in order to be effective, services must not only encompass all three areas but must also be extended to all who need them. Accordingly, "reaching out" programs have developed, in which efforts are made to identify potential users of the services, involving most of the resources of our extremely sophisticated communications system. Formal and informal educational systems have indoctrinated young people toward commitment to human service. The churches have moved from exhorting their members to be concerned about social problems a comfortable thousand miles away to greater involvement with the problems at their own doorsteps.

   These developments have resulted in the introduction of many new groups of people into manning the systems, ranging from neighborhood aides, volunteers of all ages and levels of society, management and planning personnel, to representatives of a wide variety of knowledge areas. Staffs have become more heterogeneous and are faced with the additional need to work out relationships between many different kinds of workers.

   At the same time, the systems themselves have grown larger, older, more rigid, bureaucratic, and hierarchical in structure and thus more committed to defense of the status quo. The battles between forces pushing for change and forces defending that which is are almost universal, seen also in religion, law, medicine, nursing, social work, and education. It is a time of challenge and change—a natural outgrowth of the turbulent Sixties, which called the attention of society in no uncertain terms to the unmet needs of its members and posed the problem of learning new models of operation in order to meet these needs.

A natural result of the expansion of the human service systems has been increasing use of the tax dollar to finance services whose demands are beyond the capacity of localities to absorb. In spite of the so-called "New Federalism," involving revenue sharing and local control, this trend continues. It is the rare private institution that does not get a part of its budget from federal or state funds, and with this government funding has come a centralization of control and administration. While centralization has advantages in terms of assurance of adequacy and equality of services, it also possesses certain disadvantages that are particularly apparent because of the nature of systems themselves and the nature of the consumer.

In spite of American commitment to the fallacious absolute that "bigger is always better," there seems to be a point at which the law of diminishing returns sets in, beyond which comes not greater productivity but lesser, and this law is applicable to the massive human service systems. Apparent are an increasing amount and rigidity of structure, a proliferation of rules and regulations, and growth of a hierarchy of personnel existing in formalized, defined relationships, an increasingly growing part of which is devoted to management and administrative functions and to maintenance of the system. The evils rather than the strengths of bureaucracy seem to grow with size.

Loss of flexibility and openness to change are particularly crucial in the human service systems, because the consumers of the service are needy people. Although it is possible to make certain valid, across-the-board generalizations, all people are individuals, human need is individual need, and the individual and society are both constantly changing. If services are to remain relevant, they must be capable of change as well as adaptation to specific situations. Humanization of services is all too often a casualty in large systems, sacrificed in the name of efficiency and expediency. The consumer who deviates from the norm, who does not fit the regulation, who does not qualify for service is often the one whose need for the service is greatest. The larger the program, the greater the number of people whose individual needs go unmet because they do not fit in the designated boxes. Provision must be made for "tailoring" of systems to individuals if the program is to be effective and the consumer is not to get lost in the regulations. The challenge is to devise systems that are comprehensive enough to meet the needs of the total group and yet flexible enough so that the nonconforming individual will not fall between the regulations. The individual worker providing the service, doctor, nurse, lawyer, teacher, social worker, nutritionist, acts as the essential medium through which the rules can be adapted to meet unique needs and through which the service can be "humanized." Unfortunately, there is an increasing tendency toward minimization of this kind of contact, related in part to the trends we have been discussing above and in part to the efforts to adapt and use scientific knowledge and its accompanying technology as a tool in provision of service.

Use of Technology

It is a truism that every solution raises new problems; this is obvious in the current struggles to adapt the sophisticated tools of technology to collection and processing of data in human services. Potentially, these tools hold the promise of enabling their users to provide more extensive and comprehensive service, to weigh more variables and hence provide more effective service, and to evaluate results more thoroughly and more objectively and thereby improve services.

As always, however, we are involved in the ongoing process of using and learning to use tools, and in the incompleteness of this process, the individual's uniqueness may be disregarded, individual tragedies compounded, and wide-ranging programs failures in achieving their most essential goal—service to individuals. In no sense does this indicate abandonment of this pursuit; the promise it holds is great, the present achievements formidable. It does mean, however, that we need be constantly aware of the purpose of human services and the fact that science and technology are tools only, awesome and almost overwhelming in their potential for power but controllable by the human mind.

Accountability

In the present climate of challenge to social institutions, questions have been raised about the relevancy and credibility of the human service systems. The Seventies could be designated "the age of accountability." Accountability is demanded by critics, both within and outside of the systems, who are concerned by the increasing dimensions and severity of social problems, by the apparent ineffectiveness of old methods and programs, and by the demand for increased resources to implement these services.

In one sense, this accounting is long overdue. When human need reveals itself, it is generally of an emergency nature, and immediate steps must be taken to alleviate it. Too often, these steps have been based, not on sound theory and tested knowledge, but on the need for remedy of an immediate crisis. As new bureaucracies born out of crisis came into being, they tended to perpetuate themselves and their methods of working without much objective evaluation of the results of their efforts. With the customary euphoria of a nation of hucksters, we service providers oversimplify and oversell the results in order to secure support, and by promising more than we can deliver, we make ourselves vulnerable to attack.

As this drive for accountability promotes responsibility and as it results in better conceived and planned programs, it is a desirable and constructive development. As it creates an absolute and equates results with cure or with concrete, statistically significant entities, it is less useful as applied to human services. The nature of humanity is such that it is never problem-free, and there is no human service that can create this state. Accepting this and prompting definition and limitation of goals and the development of soundly devised measurements of progress toward them is a necessary step in the long search for a more effective way of dealing with the problems inherent in being human.

If we can accept the interdependence of life forms, if we can consider that at no time in any life can an individual operate without some degree of dependence on others, then the limitations of achievement in human service are less difficult to face. If we could create the optimum social conditions, provide all the resources necessary for maximum development of human potential, and attain universal social justice, there would doubtless still remain, roughly, three groups of needy people: (1) those who need comprehensive, ongoing care to sustain life; (2) those who, with help, can improve their ability to function but will require continuing special provision of help; and (3) those who need temporary service from time to time but can assume major responsibility for their own lives. The social contract involves a commitment to provide services in all these categories, and realistically, there are many people for whom extensive ongoing service will be necessary throughout life. Accountability as responsibility is highly desirable in human service systems; accountability interpreted as demanding an absolute in terms of success mitigates against the flexibility necessary to adapt to ongoing human need.

Consumer Involvement

One of the most promising trends in modern human services is the emergence of consumers as vital participants throughout the systems: pinpointing need, planning, delivering services, and evaluating. This increased implementation of two basic philosophical values—(1) that people have a need and a right to be involved in decision-making on matters pertaining to their own welfare and (2) that fundamental change cannot be imposed from without, that there must be participation of the individual and/or social system that is changing—has been expedited by both the social unrest of the Sixties and the movement toward self-actualization that has become a pervasive part of the total social picture in the Seventies. This outlook is found not only in "open" institutions but also in traditionally authoritarian settings, hospitals and correctional and custodial institutions, and has added a much-needed dimension to the provision of service.

There are, naturally, struggles involved in implementation of this trend requiring change, both in people and in institutions. Basic policy changes do not come easily; communications among people who proceed from markedly differing frames of reference are fraught with difficulty; change and demand for learning new ways can be threatening. But, in spite of all these factors, movement in the direction of more democratic operation continues and, in general, is a source of strength and growth in human service systems.

Entry into Politics

An obvious outgrowth of consumer involvement has been the increasing politicization of service systems. The kinds of fundamental changes taking place require revision of old laws and adoption of new ones; learning the meaning and use of political structure and power; and use of collaboration and communication in order to build support and influence the underlying value systems on which action is based. It is the rare human service system today that does not use both official and unofficial channels to work in the political arena. Organized consumer groups are an increasingly significant part of the total scene.

Changing Use of "Community"

The natural outgrowth of these changes and a significant contribution to them has been the changing understanding of the meaning and use of "community." As we have begun to perceive and understand the interrelationships of all systems, both within the individuals and of people in the aggregate, we have begun to develop the knowledge and skills for working with the totality rather than the part.

More and more, we are working in and as a part of the community, rather than removing and isolating the nonfunctioning member from it. As we have understood the process of adaptation, we have learned that adaptation to long-time isolation and institutionalization is not the best preparation for return to membership in an open society. As we have understood the strength of a heterogeneous society and of the unique small group or "tribe," we are learning not only to tolerate but to promote and utilize group and individual differences to the advantage of the whole.

Emergence of Teamwork

It is obvious that service programs of the current magnitude and complexity require wide variety as well as a significant degree of knowledge and skill. It is equally obvious that no one individual can encompass the needed range and depth, that no one person can be all things to even one other person. One of the ways in which the human service systems are endeavoring to accommodate this demand for comprehensive service is through use of teams, people possessed of different specialized areas of knowledge and skill working together. Unfortunately, designating a group of people as a team does not automatically insure their ability to work as a team.

The task, then, is to study and master teamwork itself. What is a team? Who should be members? What is the relationship between the members? How can it work effectively? It is here we must begin.

Related Readings

Bell, David: The Coming of Post Industrial Society. New York: Basic Books, 1973.

A provocative "venture in social forecasting," in which the author looks at the future in light of current trends.

Bennis, Warrne; Benne, Kenneth; Chin, Robert, eds.: The Planning of Change. New York: Holt, Rinehart, Winston, 1969.

Good reference; well-organized and annotated collection of articles on all aspects of social change.

Fromm, Erich: The Revolution of Hope—Toward a Humanized Technology. New York: Harper and Row, 1968.

An outstanding humanist looks optimistically at the dehumanizing aspects of technology.

Merton, Robert: Social Theory and Social Structure, enlarged edition. New York: Free Press, 1968.

Basics of social theory as expressed by one of the pioneer thinkers in this area.

Piven, Francis and Cloward, Richard: Regulating the Poor. New York: Random House, 1971.

Consideration of the role of the poor in modern society and the part played by the human services in defining and maintaining this role.

Reissman, Frank and Popper, Hermine: Up From Poverty—New Career Ladders for Non-Professionals. New York: Harper and Row, 1968.

A look at the changing definition of professional and the role of the indigenous worker from outside the professions.

Shepard, Paul and McKinley, Daniel: The Subversive Science. Boston: Houghton Mifflin, 1969.

Highly readable collection of essays about man and his society that promotes a broad outlook at the human condition.

Toffler, Alvin: Future Shock. New York: Random House, 1970.

Thought-provoking best seller that centers around the rapid changes in modern society and the problems of adaptation.

Wilensky, Harold and LeBeaux, Charles: Industrial Society and Social Welfare. New York: Russell Sage Foundation, 1965.

Good basic background material that builds a foundation for understanding Bell's book.

CHAPTER 2

THE EVOlViNq TEAM CONCEPT

Use of an informal team in practice in human service is probably as old as the provision of such service, itself. Galen and Hippocrates had their assistants; Hamurabbi doubtless had a clerk. In his graphic portrayals of nineteenth-century orphanages, Dickens invariably presented a venal male administrator supported by an equally sordid female, each with his or her own task and role. Based on the fundamental idea of division of labor—each doing that for which he is best-prepared and best-suited and pooling the results, for the achievement of a common purpose—the concept of teamwork is evolving into a dynamic, multifaceted entity, the complicated nature and demands of which we are only beginning to examine and understand. Our use of teams has been based on learning about relating to and working with people, derived from experience and folk knowledge rather than a body of tested theories and principles. At the present time, we are both using and learning to use teams, hoping to realize their maximum effectiveness.

Because ongoing development and change are so much a part of responsible teamwork at this time and because of the danger inherent in our glib tendency to label any aggregate of workers a "team," the worker who approaches team practice and the human service system contemplating adopting it should do so with three basic principles constantly in mind.

First, there is no one model of teamwork that can be considered the ultimate model. Many different models are being used and tested. Yet, there are valid generalizations that can be made at this time about all teamwork on the basis of what we have learned.

Second, flexibility, open-mindedness, and adaptability are particularly important in both workers and systems working with models of teamwork. At this stage in its development, sound objectivity in evaluation is mandatory, so that new approaches are not abandoned without adequate testing and, conversely, are not adhered to when it is obvious that they can be modified for greater effectiveness.

Third, teamwork is not the preferred mode of service delivery in all situations. This seems so obvious it is hard to understand why it is necessary to stress it, and yet because teamwork is the "in thing" at the moment (perhaps because of our national obsession with team sports), the label is being applied indiscriminately, across the board, to all group efforts. The danger inherent in this, as pointed out in the Introduction, is that efforts to use the total approach may be abandoned in discouragement over failures that might have been foreseen. Human service workers share a common need for quick and final solutions. Generally, they also possess a commitment to humanity and a desire both to relieve suffering and to succeed in their professional endeavors, and they are under social pressure to produce these answers. The cumulative effect of these factors all too often results in fadishness. Use of the team model holds too much promise at this stage in our understanding and development of ways of working with people to fall victim to such forces.

The Age of the Specialist and the Search for Holism

Teamwork has achieved its present prominence in delivery of human services as the result of a natural ideological evolution, based on the fundamental social and systems changes considered in Chapter 1. The development and systematization of knowledge about people resulted, briefly, in the age of the autonomous expert—the specialist in a particular area operating independently, with responsibility for total service. With the proliferation of knowledge and the realization that encompassing its totality was far beyond a single individual, the need for limitation of knowledge areas became obvious.

New specializations grow, in a sloughing off process, from the original ones, thus specialty boundaries are in continuous redefinition. Medicine and its related fields offer an excellent demonstration of this process; nutrition and nursing have each developed unique bodies of knowledge and skill, consisting, in part, of content formerly within the purview of the physician. In addition to new specializations, technicians and paraprofessionals develop around the specialist, who is thus freed to spend more time with that part of the field in which only he, with his highly sophisticated expertise, is competent.

At the same time that proliferation of knowledge was creating the need for specialization, a fundamental change was taking place in the basic manner of thinking about humanity that had a significant implication for utilization of specialized knowledge in an integrated fashion in human services. Scientists, theologians, philosophers—theoreticians and practitioners alike—moved toward a perception of the world as "an integrated whole of organized complexity" that could only be adequately understood and dealt with by a holistic approach, taking into consideration the total pattern, the critical elements within that pattern, and the simultaneous relationship of continuous transaction with each other. An essential ingredient of holism is the so-called "process theory." Process theory attempts to describe what goes on in what Phillip Slater has called "the space between things"—the dynamic process of relationship among the parts.*

Holism and process theory have real advantages for the human services worker. Placing renewed emphasis on the wholeness and oneness of people and the world leads to development of ways of dealing with the problems that have arisen from fragmentation of both knowledge and practice, from overdifferentiation and under-integration. It points a way out of the trap into which the human services had fallen—attempting to work with a part of man, virtually

*Philip Slater, *The Pursuit of Loneliness* (Boston: Beacon Press, 1970).

ignoring except for lip service, the impact of the environmental forces impinging on his life field.

Most important of all, however, is that this is a dynamic theory, concerned with vital processes that are ongoing and concerned with the present and the future rather than with the past. Although it is obvious that decisions are made on the basis of past experience plus our conception of the possibilities of the future, it is not without reason that social service workers have been accused of leaning too heavily on what has been rather than on what is and what can be. If we achieve a valid understanding of an ongoing process, we can not only work in the present but also prognosticate the future and capitalize on its promise.

In human services, it is necessary not only to understand what goes on in the life fields of the clients, but also to understand what goes on in our working relationships with each other. This holistic emphasis in theory and the growing knowledge of the process involved in relationships between the unique parts of wholes can be applied not only to the systems *with* which we are working but also to the systems *in* which we are working. It should enable us to use a team model, a whole made up of parts in a process of transaction, to achieve more comprehensive conceptions than are available to any single discipline represented therein.

Processes of Working Together

Historically, three processes have been described and used to facilitate the necessary relationships between the specializations in human services: consultation, referral, and collaboration. The terms have unique meanings and have served as linkages in a highly compartmentalized framework, wherein there has been little conscious effort, except in special settings, to develop and utilize the added dimension of the *gestalt*—that almost mystic quality of wholes that is more than the sum of their parts.

These three processes, as with all the dynamic elements in working with people, are being subjected to ongoing study to determine what is actually involved in their operation and how they can be controlled and improved. All are major aspects of the developing concept of teamwork and, as such, require consideration.

Consultation

Consultation in human services can be defined as "the process of asking and receiving expert advice or information." It is generally considered to possess five major characteristics.

First, *consultation deals with a current problem or problems.* Because of a person's need for help with a problem beyond his power to solve, a consultant (a person possessing the authority of knowledge) is asked to intervene with advice or information. Consultation has a dual goal: to enable the user to deal with the immediate situation and to help him learn how to deal with future situations. The problems for which consultation is appropriate may derive from a variety of sources, in the service worker, in the client, or in the institutional setting and its program. Help given may involve the development of new insights or new skills; dealing with a crisis in worker or client; or facilitating change in the service system itself, particularly in the areas of communications, role conflicts, personal difficulties, or the authority structure.

Second, *consultation is temporary,* although in certain situations the consultant may return at various times. The consultant's role is to enable people to use themselves and their systems more effectively, and consultation accomplishes this either through the provision of knowledge or through freeing individuals from the domination of those forces that make maximum use of self impossible.

Third, *consultation is advisory*; the consultant does not implement his recommendations. His job is to provide the tools the user needs to deal with the situation himself. Although the consultation may be ongoing in the sense that the consultant will return to it from time to time, this is done not so that the consultant can take over and perform the work but so he can evaluate what is happening from a different perspective and afford continuing advice.

Fourth, *it is generally considered desirable that the consultant come from outside the service system* in which he is affording consultation, although with the increasing complexity of the systems and great diversity of specializations involved in them, it is becoming more and more possible for a consultant from within the system to possess the different perspective and objectivity that are the invaluable aspect of the process. When the consultant comes from outside the system, he or she must penetrate the field far enough to carry on work but not so far as to become personally involved in the problem situation.

Fifth, *it is considered mandatory that the consultant not possess administrative authority in the service system.* The consultant who enters a situation where there is an unsolved problem is subject to great pressures, and when he possesses administrative responsibility in the same system, there is often an incompatibility of roles that makes it difficult for him to function adequately.

The techniques used by consultants are basic to the problem-solving process: assessment, consideration of alternatives of intervention, establishment of appropriate relationships, action, and evaluation of what has been done. There is a definite educational goal in consultation, but the process used will depend to a large extent on the nature of the problem involved and on the purpose of the consultation.

Collaboration

Collaboration, which Webster has defined as the process "in which two or more workers labor together" differs from consultation in that the workers involved have a joint responsibility for carrying out an agreed-upon action. As practiced, collaboration exists on a continuum; collaborators share in planning and deciding what is to be done as well as in acting.

On one end of the continuum, we have the collaborators, each of whom is essentially autonomous, working within a specifically defined area, in a parallel manner. The necessary communication across these two parallel positions is formal, limited, and defined, and the parameters of the areas of the two or more practitioners involved are often jealously guarded. On the other end of the continuum, we have what has been defined as an integrative practice, characterized by united effort, greater flexibility of boundaries, and freedom to exchange roles and responsibilities according to need.

These two positions represent the extremes, but both exist, as do the various levels of collaboration in between. The basic philosophical stance of the collaborators, the nature of the specializations involved, and the demands of the specific situation tend to weight the process toward one end or the other of the continuum. In all cases, however, collaboration implies a sharing of planning and action, with joint responsibility for outcome.

Referral

Referral, the process of enabling a person to move on to utilize another resource, is an increasingly important aspect of human services, as they become more complex and more diversified. The very process of learning what resources are available in an increasingly complicated world is formidable, both for workers and clients. Successful referrals are based not only on this comprehensive knowledge of what is available and how to reach it but also on the basis of a differential diagnosis of both individuals and the systems involved as to what they can and cannot do.

Study of the process has indicated that the blanket referral, the offhand referral, the referral not based on assessment of the unique situational factors has little chance of being successful in enabling the persons involved to locate and make use of the appropriate resource for help. The referring person has choice of a wide range of techniques, verbal and nonverbal and involving use of various communications media; the choice must be based on the unique situation.

Combining the Three Processes

Problems in using these three processes, consultation, collaboration, and referral, are not necessarily inherent in the processes themselves but in the ways in which they are used. Clear channels of effective communication are always essential. In consultation, the fact that the practitioner is carrying out the recommendations of another specialist is an added dimension; those recommendations are filtered through another person or system, which may be quite different in both value base and ways of working from the consultant, and the recommendations that come through may not always be valid.

All three processes are integral to team practice, which arose, in part, from the need for and existence of them. All three involve utilization of differences to achieve more complete and meaningful totals. The team affords a structured forum, in which these differences can be recognized, defined, and combined through mutual effort to the greater "nourishment and expansion of each and the development of more comprehensive conceptions than are available to any single one."

Definition of Teamwork

Earlier, it was pointed out that the term "teamwork" is being very loosely used in current human services and has a variety of meanings. It is a highly flexible concept at this point, and definitions accordingly vary, but there are valid generalizations that can be made about it. The definition used here represents an effort to create a framework of the general principles that are basic to all teamwork.

> A team is a group of people each of whom possesses particular expertise; each of whom is responsible for making individual decisions; who together hold a common purpose; who meet together to communicate, collaborate, and consolidate knowledge, from which plans are made, actions determined and future decisions influenced.

The following paragraphs examine this definition.

A team is a group. As such, the members individually and totally are subject to all of the pressures and forces that operate within a group. The team constitutes a system and partakes of the basic characteristics of systems. It is a whole made up of interrelated parts, existing in a state of dynamic balance. Change in any one part of that system requires compensatory change in the others. In addition to these internal relationships, each team is involved in relationships with the other systems that make up its environment.

A team is made up of individuals who bring to teamwork individual personalities, patterns of relating to others, and ways of working, including all the essential elements of practice: values, knowledge, and skill. The individual makeup of team members will exercise tremendous influence on the nature and effectiveness of the team. It is a difficult dual task to work both as individuals and as team members.

Members of a team hold a common purpose. This is the glue that holds the team together, that provides the focus and direction to the work. Obviously, clear definition and mutual understanding of purpose are of paramount importance, although there may be, and usually is, difference of opinion as to how this purpose can be realized.

Team members communicate, collaborate, and consolidate knowl-edge, on the basis of which action is taken. This is the transactional process, out of which evolves a totality that is greater than that which can be achieved by any of the individuals working alone or alone in summation.

Individuals as Members

The degree and the manner in which team members act as individuals and as a group are highly significant. Three levels of such operation are discernible at present.

1. There are teams made up of highly skilled specialists, who practice autonomously and use the team structure to coordinate the results of their work. This can be illustrated by a group of researchers operating in the College of Agriculture of a major state university. The specialists represent veterinary medicine, pathology, microbiology, virology, biochemistry, and parasitology. Each individual does his research, alone, but all meet to discuss and coordinate the results of the individual studies.

2. Some teams are made up of a group of people with varying degrees of knowledge and skills, whose collaboration is directed toward the planning and delivery of service. An example would be the team in the institution for the mentally ill whose purpose is to provide a therapeutic milieu. This team may consist of psychiatrists, social workers, recreational therapists and physiotherapists, psychologists, nurses, ward aides, and volunteers.

3. Teams are made up of a highly integrated organization of individuals, who may or may not represent different disciplines, whose operation is as a team rather than as individuals. This model is evident in the three-person therapeutic team—the members jointly lead a sensitivity group, each performing a different role by design.

Team Types

Use of individuals on teams on all three levels is pervasive throughout human service systems at the present time, although they are probably more frequently found in complex organizations, such as medical settings. Here specialists, each with clearly defined boundaries of knowledge and skill, practice, but the contributions of many different experts are essential to achievement of the purpose of the organization.

Early teams in the health field tended to be organized around a central figure—in this instance, the physician—whose status and authority determined the operation of the team and the use of the other specialists who practiced in proximity to him. Horwitz calls this a "leader-centered team" and differentiates it from a "fraternally oriented team."* He sees this central figure as holding control on the basis of charisma, organizational support, and professional authority. In such a team, the leader makes decisions, routines tend to be bureaucratic, evaluation centers with the leader, and the team's stability depends on the leader's continuation in his role.

The fraternally oriented team is a team of equals who operate on the basis of common decision. Its work is generally more informal, its structure less rigid, its communication usually oral rather than written, and its leadership on a revolving basis.

Both types of teams are seen in current practice and are appropriate in particular situations, although there is some question, in light of what we currently know about group dynamics, of whether the leader-centered team represents maximum utilization of the team model.

Recent Developments in Teamwork

Two developments that have taken place within the last century have contributed to a change in the total climate and organization of team operations.

The first is small group research and its application to team operation. With its emphases on the egalitarian status of group members, on discussion and consensus as a way of reaching group decisions, and on democracy as the fundamental underlying principle of effective group organization, small group research is pushing toward modification of the more rigid authoritarian models. Original research on the significance of participatory democracy in producing maximum individual and group functioning as demonstrated in studies of autocratic, laissez-faire, and democratic groups has been supported by extensive subsequent studies. While it is undoubtedly the most difficult form of group operation, requiring

*John J. Horwitz, *Team Practice and the Specialist* (Springfield, Ill.: Charles C. Thomas, 1970), pp. 23–24.

the greatest maturity and self-involvement on part of the participants, it also appears to insure the greatest results.

The second recent development with major effect on teams is the so-called "new professionalism," which stresses the importance of knowledge and skill other than that based on theoretical learning. The subsequent introduction into practice of workers whose qualifications derived from experiential learning, the impact of the ballooning self-help movements, and the challenge of the effectiveness of professionals in human services have had major effect on development and use of team models and have posed problems that have to be dealt with. The main problem centers around integration of such a wide variety of practitioners into a democratic team model and development of complementary and supplementary role definitions for them.

It is unfortunate that the apparently common human tendency to seek "the" way and then become polarized around it operates here, as elsewhere, to the detriment of the whole. Effective human service rests on the combination of self-help, the assistance of workers with limited academic learning but practical skills, and the highly sophisticated knowledge and skill of the professional. The absence of any one of these three elements diminishes the whole, and the real problem lies not in opting for "either/or" but in working out the most effective combination of all.

In the reality of present-day team organization and functioning, the question of professional/nonprofessional seems to be increasingly unimportant. The significant factor lies in the possession of knowledge and skill and in suitability for performance of a specific task designated by the team. Regardless of the defined structure, there is usually negotiation taking place within the team itself regarding role, status, and definition of tasks.

The trend toward development of teams seems to be preponderately toward the "institutionalized team," prescribed by the administrative setup, with general outline of structure and roles defined, although these are almost always subject to some negotiation and change by the team itself. Teams are also being developed by practitioners or by a single important person in the setup who perceives a need to pull others who possess varying expertise into the operation. Teams may also originate from social pressures arising in the recipients of service, who see the need for additional specialized work.

The Current Status of Teamwork

At present, the proponents of team practice in human service see assets as well as liabilities in its use. Major assets can be defined in the following terms:

1. Demand for the services of certain specialists outstrips supply, particularly in certain areas, such as medicine, and team practice affords a medium for wider use of their expertise than does individual practice.

2. Team practice affords an opportunity for greater use of paraprofessionals in close relationship with the professionals, whose core knowledge they are supporting.

3. Team practice is an experience in participatory learning for team members.

4. Team practice not only increases the effective use of specialized knowledge but also provides a more comprehensive but integrated range of service.

5. Team practice promotes focus on total problems rather than on segments, as well as thinking about how the parts fit together into the whole.

6. In order to coordinate specialized knowledge, teams must focus on goals that provide a necessary direction for mutual efforts, thereby producing more meaningful work.

7. The team provides a forum for examination and evaluation of ideas in light of the differing frames of reference of the various members.

8. The process of team practice possesses "emergent" qualities, which lead to self-actualization and self-renewal. It is a dynamic procedure, promoting personal and group growth.

The major liabilities in team practice as presently used are the following:

1. Participatory democracy tends to be cumbersome and slow-moving, and team practice, in so far as it is a democratic form of operation, may partake of these characteristics.

2. In team practice, there is frequently less contact with the client or consumer of the service, as workers are operating in the interest *of* him, rather than *with* him.

3. There are major problems of communication in teams, which limit the effectiveness of the work.

4. Teamwork often seems to lead to greater rather than less fragmentation of service.

5. Team meetings are often more time-consuming for busy specialists than are consultation and referral outside the team framework.

6. The tensions that exist between various disciplines and the lack of clear definitions of boundaries of knowledge and expertise often make teamwork extremely difficult.

7. Problems in role definition are very great, and overlap is frequent.

8. Some workers on all levels in human services are not only not committed to teamwork but are poorly equipped for it.

9. The team situation fosters undesirable competition.

10. Differences in status among team members and inequities in regard for service frequently make team practice difficult.

In assessing the relative weight of these various assets and liabilities in team practice, it would seem that they might better be designated as the "potentials" and the "problems." Team practice is not completely formulated as yet. We are only beginning to recognize the real, complicated nature of the process and to be able to designate these possibilities and the unsolved problems inherent in it. On the basis of what we know at present, existence of the potentials has been demonstrated to an extent that justifies further experimentation and further effort to deal with the problems, in terms of both the human element involved and the process itself.

Related Readings

Beggs, David: Team Teaching, Bold New Venture. Bloomington, Ind.: University of Indiana Press, 1968.
   Application of principles of teamwork in education.
Browning, Douglas, ed.: Philosophers of Process. New York: Random House, 1965.
   Collection of writings of the leading process theorists, particularly useful as foundation reading in ideas about the self-renewing and emergent qualities of process.
Caplan, Gerald: Concepts of Mental Health and Consultation. Washington, D.C.: U.S. Dept. of Health, Education & Welfare, 1959.
   Concrete discussion of consultation and collaboration with input from various disciplines.
Grosser, Charles, et al: Non-Professionals in the Human Services. San Francisco: Jossey-Bass, 1969.
   Collection of useable articles on use of workers with varying levels of education in human services and the relationship demands involved.
Holmes, Oliver Wendell: The Path of the Law. Harvard Law Review, 1897, p. 475.

────── and Dewey, John: Logical Method and Law. Cornell Law Quarterly, 1924. Holmes's concepts regarding interpretation of the law and Dewey's comments illustrate the social philosophy underlying the forces operating in law and education in the early twentieth century.

Howard, John R.: Social Movement and Social Change in America. Philadelphia: J.B. Lippincott, 1974.
A look at the changing social trends and patterns developing in selected minority groups.

Lewin, Kurt: Field Theory in Social Science. New York: Harper and Brothers, 1951.
Pioneer study of relationships among the parts that make up the wholes in social functioning.

Parker, Albert A.: The Team Approach to Primary Health Care. Berkeley: University of California, 1972.
One of the many publications in the health care field dealing with teamwork, an area where much of the pioneering in its use has been done.

Romanyshyn, John: Social Welfare, Charity to Justice. New York: Random House, 1971.
Text in social welfare written from the point of view of the changing attitudes that influence the way it develops.

Slater, Phillip: The Pursuit of Loneliness. Boston: Beacon Press, 1970.
Beautifully written small book analyzing the destructive and divisive forces in American Society.

CHAPTER **3**

The individual
AS A TEAM MEMBER

"What you are speaks so loudly I cannot hear
what you say," Emerson is quoted as saying.
Realizing the validity of this statement in working
relationships as well as in personal ones and its
basic importance in human services in particular
has had tremendous impact on the preparation of
practitioners. Initially, inquiry into the "what you
are" was directed toward the consumer of the
service, but with increasing understanding of the
inescapable transactional nature of all relationships, the need for scrutiny of the practitioner's
personality structure and needs also became obvious. The added relationship dimensions and demands imposed by the team model of practice
make the need for knowledgeable use of self even
more important. Without awareness of what we
are and therefore of what we are communicating,
we experience inexplicable barriers not only in
dealing effectively with our fellow practitioners
but also in becoming that "collectivized" individual of tomorrow visualized by current theoreticians.

The individual is first, last, and always an individual. As such, he is involved in living out his own unique genetic code as it develops in a transactional process with his environment. In this process, he develops both an image of himself and a set of attitudes and behaviors for his various roles. At any given point in time, he represents both the end result of the developmental and socializing processes that have taken place within him since birth and the beginning point for the changes that will inevitably occur in the future. Although, sadly, individuals sometimes appear to be frozen into a mold as rigid as those million-year-old mammoths found in the glaciers of Siberia, this is an illusion, in light of our knowledge that life is a dynamic process and that living organisms cannot be static. The potential for personal change and growth is a vital part of the working armament of the human service practitioner, particularly as his client—both people and social institutions—are constantly shifting and being transformed in response to their own internal and external pressures.

The Team vs. the Individual

The ability to be comfortable and function in a highly fluid situation and to be open to change in self as a person and as a worker is of particular importance for the practitioner who is part of a team, especially if that team is attempting to maximize the emergent qualities of the model. As in democracy, individual participation in teamwork requires personal commitment and maturity, self-discipline, flexibility, capacity for give-and-take, willingness and ability to learn, basic respect for the other fellow with all of his differences, and the ability to examine oneself in relationships with other people with a degree of objectivity.

Carl Rogers comments:

> The immature person cannot permit himself to understand the world of another because it is different from his own and therefore threatening to him. Only the individual who is reasonably secure in his own identity and selfhood can permit the other person to be different, unique and can understand and appreciate the uniqueness.*

*Carl Rogers, *Freedom to Learn* (Columbus, Ohio: Charles E. Merrill, 1969) p. 96.

Teamwork is not only demanding on the participants, it can be time-consuming and ponderous, and emergency situations may require a shortcutting of the process and substitution of more authoritarian action. Teamwork is also vulnerable to a constant push toward elitism and abuse of power, which lends veracity to the statement that the price of democracy is eternal vigilance; the battle is never finished. However, it is generally accepted and supported by research findings that increasingly responsible and superior practice results from adoption and use of democratic principles. While the demands on the worker may be greater, the potential results apparently justify the effort.

The individual practitioner brings to the team both his personal self and his working self. While the characteristics of the latter are more apparent in work settings, it is impossible to disregard the former, particularly in the close confines of team practice. Personal self/working self can never be really separated, except for purposes of examination, and each affects the other constantly. The basic human needs for security, opportunity for growth, and meaningful relationships with others find expression in work, as well as in other aspects of life. The individual uses his unique personal characteristics to affect his work, and these attitudes and behaviors can be an asset or a liability, both to him and to the group. The accompanying cartoon (Figure 1) illustrates some underlying personality patterns of group members which determine to a large extent the role played by the individual within the group.

The Team Worker's Background

Traditionally, human service practitioners have not been well-equipped for collaborative efforts and team practice. Studies of the origins, characteristics, and aspirations of human service personnel indicate that they are largely drawn from the middle-class and are carriers, often unconsciously, of the dominant value system of that class, with its emphasis on upward mobility and personal achievement and with lip service given to interdependence as a basic essential of living and collaboration as necessary for survival. Their social milieu is also strongly success- and status-oriented, and this success tends to be measured in terms of individual achievement. In addition, stress on leadership roles in both formal and informal education

Figure 1. Personalities on a Team

programs is poor preparation of young people for positions as responsible followers.

Initially, the introduction of indigenous workers—representatives of the poor and minority groups, people drawn from other than the predominantly middle-class group—into practice of human services seemed to promise a dilution of middle-class value orientations. Unfortunately, the definition of a Republican as a Democrat whose mortgage is paid is equally descriptive of what happens with upwardly mobile human service workers.

All too frequently, the middle-class need and drive for rewards and status blunt the impact of other processes of acculturation and thus increase rather than dilute the fierce competition for individual achievement that characterizes a schizophrenic society, giving lip service to collaboration and assiduously practicing mindless competition.

The concept of the "career ladder" and the fact that status and rewards become greater as the worker climbs this ladder contribute to development of a mind set encouraging upward movement regardless of its desirability. It is particularly unfortunate in the human services, whose total rationale for existence is service delivery, that competent workers—teachers, clinicians, social workers, nurses—feel impelled to move into administrative positions according to the Peter principle, which states that the worker advances until he reaches the level where he performs incompetently and there he remains forever. Efforts have been made for years to equalize salaries and status with minimal success, but until this is done, there will be little incentive for the worker to remain a good clinician instead of becoming a poor administrator.

Positive and Negative Aspects of Teamwork

Career choices are determined in large part by personal needs, and a major motivating factor in selection of human services as a career has been the opportunity they provide for working with other individuals. This tendency has been fostered by a burgeoning awareness of the meaningfulness of individual human relationships in achieving a full life and of the personal rewards over and beyond the monetary and status ones of work directly with people. The fact that our mobile, technological, and increasingly paranoid society tends to exacerbate the problems in developing these relationships outside an extremely limited circle helps to increase the number of people who look for such relationships in their work and to increase the number of close relationships between worker and client in one-to-one contacts.

In addition, the practice models that have been developed in human services rest strongly on individual relationships. They provide a channel through which services can be provided and utilized and change can take place. The doctor/patient, teacher/student, lawyer/client, minister/parishioner, social worker/client, nurse/patient dyads are traditional and can be a source of satisfaction and fulfillment for both participants. Practice in all these areas is a combination of both science and art, and the element of artistry has been expressed in the manner in which the practitioner uses his knowledge and himself in his relationship with the person using his service. As long as knowledge was simple and limited in scope and as long as demands for service were not numerically overwhelming, these primary relationships were possible. Methods were based on them, educational and training programs stressed them, practice roles were defined in terms of them. One of the great sources of frustration for people who have been in practice for any length of time and who are a product of this tradition is not only the numerical limitation of these kinds of relationships but also the fact that they are equipped with knowledge and skills developed to meet the demands of practice models that are no longer universal.

The team worker must find his satisfactions and his motivations for effort in doing "for" rather than "with" his clients and in facilitating the achievement of his fellow workers, which then becomes a measure of his personal success. He must be able to share his clients with others and submerge his needs for dominance and leadership in the greater satisfaction of group achievement. He must be willing and able to work with the decisions of the group when they run counter to his own needs and opinions, as well as when they coincide with them. A good team offers opportunities for development of collegial relationships to a high degree, but these satisfy different needs in a different manner than do the old worker/client relationships.

The readiness and capacity of an individual practitioner for teamwork will be determined also by the manner in which he is able to deal with some of the personal insecurities fostered by the unique demands of such practice. The team worker is being asked to perform in a public arena in a way that is not demanded in individual practice. His insecurity may center around several elements:

1. The uncertainties: there is no one "right way" in team practice; the team develops its own ways out of its own strengths, and the individual is a part of this development. But if he is highly rigid and dependent on a set routine of procedures, this attribute of the team model, which may demand new roles, may cause considerable discomfort.

2. The differences in the team members: these people are designated as colleagues but vary greatly in attitudes and values, abilities, job preparation, status and rewards, as well as total personalities.

3. The self-revelation and the need for communication with others: to deal openly with hostility and competitiveness may be frightening.

4. The peer scrutiny and evaluation of the worker as a person, as a team member, and as a worker: this may involve not only feelings of personal inadequacy but also real question as to whether colleagues with different background and training are competent to evaluate specialized performance.

5. The submergence of self into the group and the necessity for sharing and collaboration: in spite of the essential factor of specialization, this may be seen as a loss of uniqueness and creativity.

6. The authority of the group to make decisions that are binding on the members.

The capacity of the team member to deal with these components will be dependent in large part on what he brings to team practice in both aspects of his self/worker dyad. It is important to remember that these two aspects of the person will be complementary if maximum functioning and personal fulfillment are to be realized. The quiet and not-so-quiet desperation that characterizes so many lives often arises from lack of this fundamental unity—the individual finding himself tied into a working situation that meets none of his fundamental human needs except that of supplying the basic necessities of life. Happily, recognition of this is increasing, and efforts are being made on all levels to provide working situations that offer satisfaction to the workers involved, not by creation of a "country club" as critics maintain, but by development of opportunities for use of worker's self in ways that meet basic human needs that cry for expression.

Cross-section of a Team Worker

In order to better understand what the individual team member brings to practice, we can examine this self/worker dyad from seven different frames of reference. It must be kept in mind that these are artificial divisions, which are constantly affecting and being affected by each other, and that the manner in which they are perceived by the remainder of the team will determine reaction to them. Figure 2 depicts these divisions.

Value System

First, the value system of the individual team member and the attitudes which derive from it are a source of both motivation and direction for his efforts in relating to other people, in working as a team member, in living. Human services *per se* rest on three fundamental values: the worth of human life, the capacity of people for change, and the ability of an outsider to facilitate change.

These values affect not only worker/client relationships but also worker/worker relationships. The worker who does not operate from these values is playing a game with himself that is fundamentally dishonest. There is a wide discrepancy, however, in the manner in which different people interpret these values and believe they should be implemented, and there are ongoing and major struggles around these

Self-Image

Values
and Attitudes

Behavior Patterns
and Norms

Latent Characteristics

Reference Groups

Generalist Knowledge
and Skill

Specialist Knowledge
and Skill

Figure 2. Cross-Section of a Team Member

differences. For example, a genetic counseling team can be caught in battle over whether to advise termination of pregnancy when sophisticated tests indicate a defective fetus. What do we mean by the worth of human life, and how does it guide our actions? Where do we draw the line between the welfare of the individual and the welfare of the society?

Behavior Patterns and Norms

Secondly, behavior patterns and the norms that support these patterns are learned and developed by a process of socialization throughout the lifetime of the worker. They represent the culture he has been and is a part of, and there are vast differences between people, concerning both norms and the behaviors these norms dictate.

An example of this is the manner in which people behave when vested with authority, a vital component of team practice. For some, possession of authority means power and control, a mandate to make decisions for others. For others, the norm requires the possessor to use authority as a tool for enabling others to participate in decision making, and the leader who so uses it would ensure that all team members are totally involved, each according to his own capacity. The behavior of the powerless person in the face of authority is an equally valid example of this: does he challenge appropriately and effectively or inappropriately and ineffectively? does he accept passively but with resentment? or does he accept this way of behaving as being the natural and desired order of things?

Latent Characteristics

Third, latent characteristics of the team member are an important but often overlooked part of the uniqueness he brings to the team. These would include such things as age, sex, race, socioeconomic standing, appearance, and religion, as well as those characteristics which derive from the specialization he represents. The perception and interpretation of these latent characteristics affect expectation and designation of roles. The dangers in stereotyping based on latent characteristics are great. The team that operates on the assumption that all female members make good secretaries will probably be sadly disillusioned, as well as in trouble with the adherents of women liberation.

Recently, an effort has been made to study and evaluate the effect that sexual differences of practitioners have on task performance, to identify the positives and negatives, if such exist, and to make conscious use of this differential to achieve greater results. An interesting development has resulted from the use of women as police officers and as therapists in team work with violent mental patients. Initial findings indicate that the presence of women on such teams has a "calming effect" on the violent person. Such studies point out the importance of latent characteristics of the worker and the fact that they need to be assessed and consciously used in developing a unified team effort.

Reference Groups

Fourth, the reference groups with whom the team member relates or aspires to relate or with whom he associates himself and feels a part constitute another aspect of his uniqueness. These identifications are made on the basis of needs of the worker, and the group with whom he identifies will do much to shape his values, attitudes, norms, and behavior. Reference groups change throughout the life experience, and this change is frequently obvious in appearance and dress as well as in other aspects of character. The new Graduate Assistant on a college faculty can be seen in the process of this change, from identification with a vital, challenging student group to identification with one of the many different faculty groups.

One of the values of the indigenous worker in human services has been his identification with the recipients of service. But this identification may be lost in the process of his absorption into the service system.

Generalist Knowledge

Fifth, the generalist knowledge and skill of the individual worker is that which he holds in common with the other team members and make it possible for him to work in such a model. While this will vary in degree as well as in usage, it is essential that he understand and be able to use communication, collaboration, and group processes, and the extent to which he does so will determine his effectiveness.

Specialist Knowledge

Sixth is the specialized knowledge and skill that the individual team member possesses, on the basis of which he has been selected for work on this particular team. In the modern concept of teaming, this may be based on experiental learning, on didactic learning, or on both. In this aspect of his preparation for human service, the specialist may hold membership in a profession which exercises control over both his behavior and his attitudes to a significant degree and will affect his ability to be a team member. A human services team may not only include representatives of different professions, but also persons without specific professional identification, and these diversities, in spite of the trend toward emphasis on competence rather than credentials, constitute assets and liabilities, depending on how they are understood and used.

A profession is an occupation with certain very specialized characteristics. These are generally recognized as:

1. The possession of a body of unique knowledge, and development of skills and techniques growing out of that theoretical knowledge.
2. Recognition by society of the profession's ability to provide special needed services, sanction of and reward for their performance, and delegation of authority to the profession to regulate itself within certain specified boundaries.
3. Acceptance by the profession of an underlying system of values, and development of a code of ethics which is binding on the members.
4. Ability to control the admission of new members.

Although professions are exclusive in the sense that they not only shut people out but also shut people in, it would be a mistake to consider them as monolithic or as consisting of a rigidly homogeneous group of practitioners. In actuality, they are heterogeneous, in terms of both groups and individuals. They are also dynamic—they change. Professions exercise control over their members through delineation of the boundaries in which they may work, through provision of guidelines for this work, through required education, and through required commitment to certain values and ethics.

Professions not only differ in the essential components of practice—values, knowledge, and skill—they also exist in a hierarchy, with the older, more established ones, such as medicine, law, and the ministry, possessing major status and the more recent ones, such as engineering, teaching, nursing, and social work, possessing lesser status. The increased amount and specialization of knowledge and the complexity of task demands in our complicated society have resulted in a proliferation of professions, each of which stakes a claim to its own area and develops its own mystique.

Somehow, a team, in order to be effective must be able to use the major differences constructively, those existing between the professions and those between the "professionals" and the "non-professionals." Learning to do this is derived both from the process of teaming itself and from educational experiences, both formal and informal.

Self-image

Finally, and of overriding importance in the individual's aptitude for teamwork, as well as in his total life experience, is his self-image: how he sees himself, both as a person and as a worker, how he feels about it, and how he uses what he sees. The individual perceives the team and other team members from this frame of reference; and, accordingly, it and they can be fulfilling, stimulating, frightening, frustrating, maddening.

To a large extent, self-image determines a person's ability to participate in interpersonal relationships. It will determine the reference groups he identifies with, the manner in which he uses his latent characteristics, the way in which he behaves and the norms of behavior he espouses, his attitudes, and the way in which he operationalizes his value system. It will have much to do with his professional or vocational choice and the manner in which he interprets and carries out the demands of his work. On the team, the individual functions as a person, a specialist, a position occupier, and a task performer, and the manner in which he fills these different slots will depend, in large part, on his image of himself in them and in his relationships with the other team members.

Six Individuals on a Team

Figure 3 illustrates individual functions in these four different aspects of team membership. Taken together, they constitute the totality of the team, a dynamic balance of relationships between different entities. Depicted is a rehabilitation team in a children's hospital, whose purpose is to provide treatment and care of children with long-term disabilities.

The People

(I) Bill Jones, M.D., is a full-time member of the hospital staff and the designated leader of the team. He is a young man, who identifies with the liberal wing of the medical profession and who, in his education, learned to work with a variety of other disciplines on the level of equality rather than on conception and perception of them as

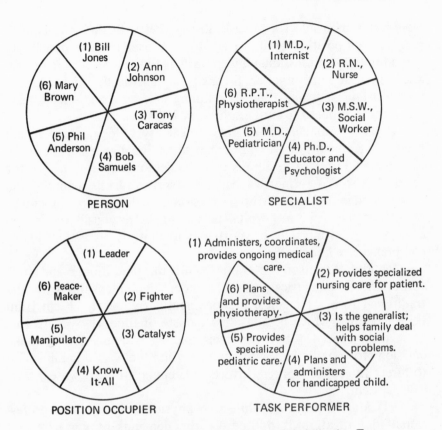

Figure 3. Four Functions of a Six-Person Rehabilitation Team

peripheral to his expertise. He is responsible for administration of the team and for coordination of its efforts with those of the other systems in the hospital. His concept of leadership is democratic, and he is sometimes hesitant to use the authority of his position.

(II) Ann Johnson, R.N., is a militant nurse, a fighter of "the system," who identifies strongly with her patients and is resentful of almost all authority. She is extremely competent and responsible in her professional role and disciplined in her behavior but will not hesitate to challenge, which she often does in such an abrasive manner that she can defeat a worthwhile objective. She is able to accept compromise but only after a strong fight.

(III) Tony Caracas, M.S.W., is the team generalist and case

manager, responsible for tying it all together with the child and his family. This position tends to cause some overlap of responsibility and adds to his professional uncertainty as to the appropriate boundaries of social work practice. Strongly humanistically oriented, he is a comfortable person, often functioning to disarm and enable team members to proceed toward a solution to differences.

(IV) Bob Samuels, Ph.D. in clinical psychology, is the recent product of a highly research-oriented educational program and tends to think in terms of absolutes that are demonstrable by use of the scientific tools. A former teacher, he possesses a happy combination of knowledge and skill in both areas, and as director of the educational program for the hospital he has major responsibility in this area. As a team member, he is often an irritant, by his assumption of comprehensive knowledge.

(V) Phil Anderson, M.D., is a private practitioner and staff consultant in pediatrics. He is an older man, identifies with the traditional form of medical practice, and is frequently absent from team meetings, which he considers a waste of time. He sees his role as medical specialist but also feels that he is competent to make decisions for rather than with the nurse and the physiotherapist and to direct the social worker's efforts in keeping with his own personal value system.

(VI) Mary Brown, a middle-aged physiotherapist, whose professional identification is diluted by the demands of her wife and mother roles. She feels a lack of status and is uncomfortable with conflict and willing to accept decisions made for her. As a team member, she seeks peace and prefers to smooth things over rather than battle out an issue. In her own field, she is unusually good, compassionate, and understanding and able to hold her patients to necessary effort in spite of fatigue and pain.

The Processes of Interaction

Out of this combination of people, a whole must be formed. A part of the uniqueness of a team is that it can and does accommodate varieties of behaviors and still be effective; its totality and balance are established on the basis of this accommodation. The team can also so constitute itself that it can work with destructive behavior on the part of a member—but only to a point. If this behavior should assume the form, for instance, of sarcastic, belittling attacks on other team members to the point that they are unable to handle them, that they are angry at the team for not rescuing them, or that they are too frightened to work effectively, then the team must take action or risk losing morale and destroying effectiveness.

A problem-solving team in human services is not and cannot be a treatment group in the pure sense, but of necessity from time to time, it will have to deal with the basic personalities of the team members and the interpersonal relationships within the team. Team structure and function can be assets in this, in that they allow for efforts toward resolution in terms of the reality-based work of the team itself. One of the major shortcomings of sensitizing experiences *per se* is that they are often divorced from reality and have to be translated from the protected setting in which they take place to the struggle of day-to-day functioning.

The member has a shared team responsibility and a total personal responsibility for his own contribution to this aspect of team life. He should be aware of the transactional nature of all relationships and alert to his own contribution to these exchanges. In the process of team interaction, he will be able to pick up feedback in the responses to the manner in which he uses himself that will alert him to what he is communicating and to whether the content and process add to or detract from his effectiveness. He needs to be open to such feedback, aware of himself as an individual and of his basic attitudes toward other people.

The instrument "Invitation to Introspection" reproduced in Appendix A can provide a starting point toward the never-finished task of developing this self-insight. If necessary, such knowledge can also be developed by participation in the seemingly boundless opportunities leading to increased sensitivity, self-awareness, and self-actualization.

Related Readings

Argyus, Chris: Integrating the Individual and the Institution. New York: Wiley, 1964.
    A study of the factors that affect the relationships between persons and social institutions.
Erikson, Erik: Childhood and Society. New York: Norton, 1950.
    Identity, Youth and Crisis. New York: Norton, 1968.

Two excellent paperbacks that can be useful in developing a theory of the human condition with emphasis on the environmental factors.

Flach, Frederic: The Secret Strength of Depression. Philadelphia: J.B. Lippincott, 1974.

Readable and useful book expounding the theory that depression associated with beginnings of new learning can be a constructive force in the life experience.

Fromm, Erich: The Art of Loving. New York: Harper and Row, 1956.

Old, but excellent treatise on self-love as related to ability to love others.

Gray, William; Duhl, Frederick and Drizzo, Nicholas: General Systems Theory and Psychiatry. New York: Little, Brown, 1970.

Emphasis on the point of view that individual characteristics are related to interactions among people as well as to internal factors.

Henry, William; Sims, John and Spray, Lee: The Fifth Profession. San Francisco: Jossey-Bass, 1971.

Proposal for unification of therapists in human services based on commonality of origin and education.

Maslow, Abraham: Toward a Psychology of Being. New York: Van Nostrand, 1968.

Humanism and optimism are the central themes of this and Maslow's other works; good background reading.

Rogers, Carl: Freedom to Learn. Columbus, Ohio: Merrill, 1969.

Readable and useful discussion of the factors involved in realization of potentials for growth within the self.

Spiegel, John: Transactions: The Interplay between the Individual, Family and Society. New York: Science House, 1972.

A look at the relationships between these three vital systems utilizing knowledge from various disciplines.

CHAPTER 4

THE iNTERNAL life of THE TEAM, I

It is naive to bring together a highly diverse group of people and expect that, by calling them a team, they will in fact behave as a team. It is ironic indeed to realize that a football team spends forty hours a week practicing teamwork for the two hours on Sunday afternoon when their teamwork really counts. Teams in organizations seldom spend two hours per year practicing when their ability to function as a team counts forty hours per week.*

This statement points up a major ongoing requirement for the effective team—to foster its own development into a mature working body. It also stresses that this requirement, on which the success of the team rests, is frequently neglected in our use of the team model in human service.

The Mature Team

Heiman defines the mature group (and a team is a specialized kind of group, whose energies are

*Wise, Beckard, Rubin, and Kyte, *Making Health Teams Work* (Cambridge, Mass.: Ballinger, 1974), page 56.

devoted to problem-solving) as one that has attained maximum inter-action, including possession of certain characteristics, enumerated as follows.

First, the mature group has a clear definition, understanding, and acceptance of its purpose and supporting goals; is capable of proceeding toward these goals in an effective, orderly fashion; and is able to anticipate and plan ahead, at the same time carrying on its day-to-day work. It deals with reality rather than fantasy and is able to develop and carry through effective problem-solving.

Second, a mature team has achieved its gestalt, the "arrangement of its separate elements in a form so integrated as to appear and function as a unit that is more than a simple summation of its parts," according to Webster. It has developed its own value system and norms of behavior. The bonding and cohesiveness that have developed are characterized by the abilities to adapt to and change with the demands of different situations, to accommodate both established ways and readiness for change, and to encourage objectivity about the team's functioning. It has created within itself a climate of psychological freedom that encourages expression of all feelings and differing points of view and provides for a unity that does not demand uniformity of thought and behavior. It is able to use conflict constructively.

Third, a mature team has developed a common language and created a pattern of effective communication, both within itself and with its environment.

Fourth, a mature team has defined the roles of its members in such a way that boundaries and overlap are clearly understood and accepted, that there is sufficient flexibility to provide for changes as necessary, and that maximum use is made of the differing abilities of the members, both latent and overt.

Fifth, a mature team has developed a flexible structure that will meet its operational needs, both tangible and intangible, yet is subject to change. It has provided for leadership that is not overdominating, for the necessary supportive personnel, for the logistical demands of record-keeping, space, etc.

Sixth, a mature team is accountable primarily to itself and secondarily to its parent organization and has thus made the necessary provision for supervision and evaluation of its work and the results thereof.

Finally, a mature team is cognizant of the emergent self-renewing qualities inherent in its work and is committed to development of them through support for creativity and innovation.

This concept of maturity carries the implication of a high degree of development, approaching perfection, but when used in thinking about vital systems it must not be treated as an absolute. It is obvious that teams, like people, are always in the process of both being and becoming and that they will need to work at these essential demands of teaming in varying degrees and manifestations throughout their life span.

The Evolution of a Team

Bullfinch's Mythology tells us that Minerva, the goddess of wisdom, leaped forth from the brain of Jupiter, "mature and in complete armour."* Unfortunately, teams are not created in the same manner, although we frequently behave as if they were. A mature team evolves by processes of give-and-take, trial-and-error, objective evaluation of what is happening, and renewed beginnings.

In order to understand and work better with these processes, theoreticians in the area of group development have visualized it in "life stages," just as the evolution of any vital system can be visualized. Use of this projection rests on the following realizations:

1. The stages are not absolute; characteristics of one will be found in others, just as the grown person may show vestiges of infancy.

2. Each stage is dependent to a degree on those that preceded it, and if the tasks inherent in a stage are incomplete or unfinished, they will probably create problems and need to be worked on later in the life cycle of the system.

3. Each team is unique and possesses unique potentials; it develops at its own rate of speed and in its own individual pattern.

4. This evolution is never completed until the team is dissolved, since such systems learn to cope with differing developmental tasks as they develop and their capacity to use this learning will determine how effectively they will be able to deal with the demands of their own growth.

Life Stages

Although organization and terminology will vary, there is general agreement on the characteristics common to each of these stages and

Bulfinch's Mythology (New York: Dell, 1967), p. 91.

on the order in which they follow each other. Based on the thinking of many different people who specialize in small group theory and practice, we can arrive at the following order and description of group stages for our own use. (See also Table 2.)

Stage I, Orientation: Determination of position with reference to the setting and the circumstances. In this stage, team members are introduced to the initial situation they will be responsible for developing. It is important in orientation that the structure be rigid enough for support but flexible enough to allow for growth. When people enter new situations, they are subject to stress—an important factor in the early stages of team development.

Stage II, Accommodation: The adaptation of the members to each other and to the team model. This is the stage in which the disparate components begin to form into a pattern of complementary parts.

Stage III, Negotiation: The transactions related to both position and task carried out, decisions made, and conclusions reached. Individual members have become part of a team yet retain their individual integrity and differentiation. Unity develops, and a working agreement is concluded.

Stage IV, Operation: Action resulting in change. This is the stage of actual team performance, in which it, having completed the initial internal organization, proceeds to deal with the external tasks, striving for achievement of its purpose.

Stage V, Dissolution: The final step. The team dissolves into its component parts, and the results of the total experience are evaluated.

It must be kept in mind that this division into stages is merely a tool for thinking, an attempt to describe what happens, and should not be taken as an absolute. Team development takes place both through these stages of development and through the content of the work experience simultaneously. The specialist who is engaged in the process of finding himself in relation both to his fellow team members and to the team model does this, in part, through use of the actual content of the work experience: through contributing his thinking, knowledge, and skill to the efforts of the whole and through receiving that of his fellow team members. Furthermore, this development is continuous and unending, because the team, itself, is dynamic and composed of parts which are all in the process of change and development.

One's initial reaction—that the process described here is unwieldly and time-consuming, that it can and should be telescoped—is understandable. This is however, only a formulation of what hap-

TABLE 2 The Life Stages of a Team

Stage	Characteristics	Member Tasks	Team Tasks	Outcomes
I. Orientation (determination of position with reference to setting and circumstances).	Definition of situation. Exploration. Learning. Evaluation.	Learn what is expected and relate this to self. Deal with lack of familiarity, anxiety, mistrust, stress.	Define boundaries. Provide supports.	Acquaintance with colleagues. Understand system. Beginning security. Beginning involvement and identification.
II. Accommodation (adaptation and arrangement to create a whole)	Manipulation. Movement and change of positions. Power struggles. Rearrangements of parts of whole.	Find appropriate place for self, both personally and professionally.	Provide structure and climate conducive to maximum freedom in and facilitation of adaptation process.	Common language and communication developing. Values and norms developing. Affiliation with team developing.
III. Negotiation (transaction and conclusion by mutual understanding).	Bargaining and concluding. Establishment of boundaries and content of specialization in relation to other specializations.	Use self as a team member—able to communicate, differ, confront, use conflict and collaboration.	Define boundaries of purpose and specializations. Establish contract. Designate goals, tasks, roles.	Dependency and differentiation established. Unity developed. Working arrangements concluded.
IV. Operation (purposeful action).	Achievement of complementarity and gestalt.	Relate to team and to individual members. Use both generalized and specialized knowledge. Reach individual decision. Perform tasks.	Maintenance of both internal and external balance and vitality. Decision making, planning and executing work.	Collaboration movement toward achievement of goals and realization of purpose.
V. Dissolution (separation into components).	Evaluation of process, problems, possibilities, and achievement in relation to purpose and goals.	Objective assessment of personal and team performance.	Support open and critical evaluation of process and results.	Personal and team change. Awareness of success/failure and appropriate use thereof.

pens; the speed with which it happens depends on the team. New or young teams and inexperienced team members may have more difficulty in dealing with this process. The old hands who understand what is transpiring can fit into the developmental flow and adapt to and facilitate its demands more easily. Ineffectualness or breakdown in teamwork is all too frequently related to incomplete or faulty team development; thus, the time involved in team development should be whatever is needed to build a firm foundation.

One of the most time-limited uses of teams in the human services is use of a team of two to four outside consultants, brought in to evaluate a program. These people are not only specialists in a particular aspect of the program, itself, but are usually experienced, knowledgeable, and well-disciplined in performing as team members. Their roles are generally clearly defined, as is the purpose and structure of the team; leadership has been designated; and it is understood at the outset that the work of the team is time-limited. In this type of group, the dynamics of team formation and development move rapidly.

Interpersonal Relationships

The above formulation of team development stresses the need of the team to deal with the relationships along its members. While it should be remembered that a team is a working group and that its major concern is attitudes and behaviors related to work, it will imperil its existence and its effectiveness by ignoring personal feelings and concerns. Teams are made up of people, not cyphers, and people are totalities and cannot be separated into parts. In its initial stages, the team must deal with the establishment of relationships, and throughout its life cycle, it must maintain them, so that they provide the clear channel through which work within the team is done. The relationship demands will vary according to the purpose for which the team exists. The type of interpersonal involvement is, of necessity, greater on a team whose purpose is therapy, which involves use of the self by the therapist. This can be illustrated by a psychiatric team of cotherapists, in which the relationship of the various members is an important part of the work itself.

In a childrens' treatment center, a team of three therapists (psychiatrist, psychologist, and social worker), dealing with the problems of a child in a grandmother-dominated home, used demonstration before a one-way mirror in a play setting to teach the three adults ways of constructively relating to each other and to the child. The internal relationship demands of this team were intense and quite different from those of the three-person consultation team noted earlier.

During its life cycle, the team will need to cope with various changes in its makeup and structure. Introduction of new members, changes imposed from without, and changes originated within the team through its own self-evaluation and normal process of maturation will demand that some of the development process be reworked from time to time.

The Beginning of Team Development

The initial meeting of the Childrens' Hospital Rehabilitation Team (presented at the end of Chapter 3) can serve to illustrate the manner in which the beginning phases of a team's life span operate. This team is provided for in the institutional table of organization. The leader is designated and the various roles are defined and the slots filled on the basis of administrative decision and assignment. It is an open team, in the sense that new slots can be created by both team and institutional recommendation.

Bill set the initial team meeting for 8 a.m., when Phil was in the hospital on rounds. Held as a breakfast meeting in a small room off the cafeteria, there was a brief period of informal, get-acquainted discussion. Everyone was on time except Phil, but he came in to grab a cup of coffee and a roll and join them just as Bill was opening the formal meeting.

Bill: We set aside just an hour for this meeting, so I think we'd better get started. Do we all know each other? (murmurs of assent) OK. Vic (administrator) has suggested that we try a more formal team setup to facilitate diagnosis and planning, both while the kids are in the hospital and at discharge. We've had considerable static from both staff and parents and some misunderstandings that seem to be based on lack of coordination—like with the Leopold child.

Phil: (blandly) I can't and won't come to a lot of meetings.

Bill: I don't think its going to mean more meetings—just more efficient and organized ones. Once we learn where each of us fits and get some ground rules established, we ought to be able to operate in our regular staffing and predischarge meetings. Actually, it should be a more economical way to work.

Phil: (skeptically) I'll believe that when I see it.

Bill: (lightly) Well, we'll try to make a believer out of you. What do the rest of you think?

Ann: (with feeling) If we can avoid a snafu like the Leopold thing, I'm all for it. The floor nurses have got to know where these kids are, and we can't have them dragged out of the wards—the routine there has to go on.

Mary: We need to coordinate our schedules better . . .

Ann: (continuing) And we can't have parents in the wards at all times. We've got to have some order.

Tony: (playing with his pipe) I guess that hits me . . . but those people were so upset that actually seeing the kid was the only thing that would help. I think we ought to be able to make exceptions. Anybody mind if I smoke?

Ann and Phil: (together) Yes!

(Everyone laughed as Tony looked startled, then joined the laughter and put his pipe aside with the comment that it was their responsibility if he went into an anxiety state.)

Bill: It sounds like we really do need to grease the wheels. How can we best start?

Bob: (pontifically) The best way to work these things out is in the actual process of working. Why don't we start with staffing on a new admission and go on from there?

Ann: I think we might make a few agreements ahead of time . . .

Bill: (quickly) Lets start there then. Can we define our purpose as a team designed to provide study, diagnosis, treatment plan, ongoing evaluation, and final disposition of a selected number of cases coming into the hospital? This would mean that we focus on them and work out the necessary decisions together. . . .

In this brief beginning, the first four steps in the formation and life stage of a team were involved. These six people had fairly clear role definitions, based on the manner of team organization and their own individual expertise. They were part of a larger organization that possessed both the advantage and disadvantage of designated channels of communication and procedures. Both the personality patterns and the inherent problems in the situation were obvious in these exchanges, but the group members had the advantage of being open and direct with each other from the outset. Bill did a good job of providing a structure yet encouraging questions and involvement from all participants. There was indication of this team's potential for vital, lively growth, with considerable conflict and meaningful collaboration.

Formation, Composition, and Structure

A maturing team moves toward becoming a social system in the sense that it is a group of people who interact within an accepted structure and according to accepted patterns in order to achieve an accepted purpose. Its health as a system is based on common agreement of the team members as to values and goals, how well it meets the needs and demands, motivation and commitment to its continuing existence, and the complementarity of roles of the various members achieved. In order to understand the team and what is transpiring therein, it is necessary to examine both the totality and the relationships between the component parts, rather than looking at any one part. All of the members are affecting and being affected by not only the other members but also by the total system. Initially, it is important to understand the circumstances of formation and selection of the various members who combine to form this totality.

Formation

Impetus for team formation in human service may arise from the setting and the parent institution, from practitioners themselves, or from the recipients of the service. In any instance, it grows out of awareness that the demands of the work to be done require use of a system, whereby a variety of specialized knowledge and skill can be brought to bear in a highly correlated fashion on the problem at hand.

At the present time in human service systems, there is a trend towards the institutionalized team, whereby the host institution recognizes appropriateness of the team model for the task at hand; sets up the requirements in terms of personnel, role designation, and structure; and provides supportive services. In such instances, the philosophical stance of the institution is of major importance in determining who will serve on the team. The institution may dictate, for example, that only particular disciplines be represented or that no representative of the consumer group be included. The realistic limitations on availability of specialists may make it necessary to adapt that which exists and use occasional consultation or the not-yet-fully exploited resources of audiovisual communication to supplement available expertise.

The major determinant in selection of team members should be the purpose for which the team is formed and the kinds of knowledge and skill needed to achieve that purpose. The team may be at a real disadvantage if the parent institution is too dominating in this respect and locks the team into limited selection of members. As the team develops, it may become apparent that new varieties of expertise are needed, and the team should be free to negotiate inclusion of additional personnel.

One interesting modern development in the use of teams is the inclusion of the consumer of the service—the client—as a team member. This is fairly widely accepted when a therapeutic milieu is being created, as in nursing homes, a terminal cancer ward, foster care. We in human services have long subscribed to the principle that basic changes come from within systems themselves, and thus maximum involvement of the systems, individuals or groups, should be a high priority. Team membership is one aspect of that involvement, and while it presents some yet unsolved problems, it also offers opportunities and is deserving of further study.

In a conservative southeastern community of 30,000, Buchannan was the only high school, thus drawing students from both urban and rural areas. The guidance counselor became concerned over rumors about the high incidence of venereal disease among the students, feeling that with so much smoke there must be some fire. Accordingly, she talked with the school superintendent, and they decided to explore further to determine the extent of the problem and possible alternatives for action. They invited the couple who were presidents of the PTA, one of the general practitioners who was a school board member, the president of the student council, and two classroom teachers to a meeting to discuss the matter. There was general agreement that although none thought the disease had reached epidemic proportions, it was of sufficient concern, in light of the overall social picture, to merit action. Out of this meeting, came the first steps in team effort directed toward developing an educational program for students, parents, and the general community.

Members were selected on the basis of particular expertise in a needed area and included the guidance counselor, the physician and school board member, a representative of the PTA, two students, and two classroom teachers. The PTA representative was appointed by the president, and the two classroom teachers selected by the superintendent on the basis of interest and what he considered their special competence for the tasks involved. There was considerable discussion of how the student representatives should be selected, and the final decision was made on the basis of the groups in the school they could represent. As the team worked together, they decided they could use the knowledge of the newly hired health planner in the county, who possessed considerable skill in community education. The team selected its own leader, and the school provided supportive services: a place to meet, secretarial service, and institutional support.

In contrast to this team, which grew out of the existence of a problem demanding various expertise and operated as a unit, is the institutionalized team in the Child Guidance Clinic mentioned earlier. That setup required that all applications for service be assigned to a team consisting of a psychiatrist, psychologist, and social worker, who would do a prescribed diagnostic workup, with contributions from each of the specialists, followed by a staff meeting, in which knowledge is pooled, decisions are reached, and recommendations are made for ongoing treatment. In some instances, the situation is returned to this team for further evaluation of treatment; in some instances, it is carried on from this point by the individual team member assigned responsibility.

Size

The size of a team is related to its purpose, to the selected ways of achieving that purpose, and to the type and degree of interaction needed. Research into group dynamics indicates that the small group has distinct advantages over the larger one in promoting maximum interaction and interstimulation, in developing responsible participation, in fostering learning by exchange and experience, and in developing and sharing leadership. It provides opportunity for greater closeness among the members, for greater development of group unity, for emergence of a sense of equality, and for group thinking and decision. While the small group has method and structure, it can still be informal and democratic.

The actual number of individuals in a small group usually varies from five to twenty, although a team of twenty is approaching the size when some of the disadvantages of larger groups begin to evidence themselves: emergence of subgroups, lack of participation and shared responsibility, increasingly dictatorial leadership.

Subgroups

In groups of any appreciable size, there is a tendency toward formation and emergence of subgroups, and teams are in no way exempt from this pattern. They may develop around a strong leader; they may be based on friendship, on similarity of professional identification, on commonness of accepted values and norms; or they may arise from a desire for supportive allies, either because of personal insecurity or to form a coalition to change or control what is happening in the team.

Whatever the reason for their formation, subgroups can be divisive and disruptive to maximum team functioning. Their development can be minimized by an open team climate and adoption of goals that are acceptable to and require committment from all team members. Once subgroups have developed, they can be controlled by a conscious effort to cut across their boundaries in setting up small task forces or working units. The team also will need to face the fact of the existence of subgroups and assess their significance in team functioning.

Formation of a subgroup based on a coalition of team members attempting to change what is happening on the team is legitimate but should be a last-resort method of change. It frequently results from inadequate or too-authoritative leadership. The team as a whole will need to look at what is happening, make a decision as to whether this is advantageous or disadvantageous, and act accordingly.

Dr. Phillips had been Chief of the Alcoholism Unit at the hospital for many years and, by virtue of his position, acted as leader of the diagnostic team which assessed all admissions and planned treatment. He operated on the basis of his record and was reluctant to change, and because of his power and the support of the administration, he was able to effectively quash all moves toward use of newer methods and techniques.

Dr. Manderson, a new Ph.D. psychologist, was instrumental in forming a subgroup based on a coalition of team members who wanted a more open team and opportunity to use different methods of treatment. When their purpose was achieved, however, members of this group resumed their primary identification with the team as a whole, rather than with the subgroup which had successfully moved the team to change.

This example shows constructive use of a subgroup. Had Dr. Manderson and his cohorts retained their identity as a splinter group in order to control the total team, they would have split the team, destroying its morale and the democratic process of team action that results in greatest productivity.

While the small group generally makes for closer and more open relationships among the members, the nature of the work being done, the clarity with which the various roles can be defined, and the boundaries of the specializations designated will affect the number of people who can work together effectively with a minimum of interactive process. A cardiac resuscitation team is an excellent example of effective use of an impersonal, large team. Where boundaries are less clear, where there is more overlap and possible duplication, and where the worker is using his personal self as a part of his working armament, the greater the need for closeness and mutual interaction of the team members.

Composition

Because a team is a dynamic unit, formation is never complete nor final. Thought needs to be given to the process involved in incorporating new members into the ongoing team, not only in terms of orientation of the new worker but also in terms of the impact of the different person on the team and its operation, regardless of whether he is filling a vacated slot or a new one. If the slot demands very specific knowledge and concrete skills, such as that of a technician operating a blood-typing machine, the impact of the worker's artistry and personality will be less important than that of, for instance, a teacher working with a deaf child.

The old controversy over whether practice in human service is science or art has generally been resolved by an understanding that it is the combination of both elements, meaning that practice will vary with the practitioner. The new team member will bring a different element to the teamwork and there must, of necessity, be a shift to accommodate his differences. Moreover, the new member in the already formed team will be entering a group in which the balance of work and relationships has been established. Of necessity, this old balance will need to be upset and a new one arrived at, based on a new complementarity.

Some believe this can only be achieved by reenacting the total life stages of a team (Table 2), and this would appear to be valid statement, although certainly the process should be less demanding in terms of both time and energy. New members provide significant new input into the team and are a source of vitality. A strong, flexible team should have little difficulty incorporating new members and benefitting therefrom. The rigid, highly structured team committed to one inflexible model will find any innovation difficult to adapt to.

There is a tendency in many institutions to employ a total team rather than hire new members for an already existent team or build one of its own. The problem is that teams, like individuals, are unique, and each has its own way of working. The institution that introduces a total, preformed, and already operating team into its system will need to be prepared to accept changes if its new team is to realize the strength and diversity that is the greatest asset of the model.

One of the major factors in group composition is the balance of homogeneity and heterogeneity that can be encompassed and yet permit development of the type of bonding among members needed for achievement of a particular purpose. A problem-solving team should comprise members whose homogeneity is such that they can accept a common purpose, communicate with each other, and work together as a stable but not static group. But it should be sufficiently heterogenous to ensure vitality and encompass the necessary variations in specialization.

Structure

Teams in human service are in the process of critically examining the range of differences in education, social status, and professional or occupational preparation that can be incorporated into an effective group. Some theorists specify that team members be drawn entirely from professionals capable of autonomous practice, who will operate on an equal level. Others postulate a rigid role stratification, in terms of supervisory responsibility by higher-level practitioners over lower-level ones. Still others prefer one central, highly specialized professional, with whom the other team members function as paraprofessionals.

The appropriateness of the use of the structure and composition of each of these three models is determined by the purpose for which the team is formed and by the practice demands involved. The team that can accommodate great heterogeneity among its members retains its capacity to use a democratic mode of functioning, which allows for maximum realization of the potential of each member and of the team, will require a structure that is clearly defined and orderly but flexible and capable of change.

Climate

The climate that prevails within the team structure is significant. Ideally it is open, safe, disciplined, and stimulating.

It is *open* in the sense that it is receptive to input from all sources and capable of processing and utilizing it. It possesses a readiness for change and a committment to use the emergent qualities of group life constructively.

It is *safe* in that contributions of all members are regarded equally; that all ideas and persons are respected; that members can question, disagree, and fight without fear of retaliation or destruction.

It is *disciplined* in that members can accept the limitations as well as the possibilities of their own knowledge and skill and that of others; that they can face and debate issues openly and objectively; that they can use the team process constructively, not to manipulate or undercut others.

Finally, it is *stimulating* in that the freedom for expression and critical evaluation of ideas, the interplay of differences, and the total dialectical process sparks creativity and promotes innovation.

The team climate that possesses these four qualities will be an enabling one, both for the individual members and for the team. As the team grows older, however, two characteristics may become apparent which will inhibit the maintenance of this climate. The first is the tendency of aging systems to become rigid, committed to maintenance of the status quo, and less open to input and feedback. Hierarchies become established and bureaucratic qualities emerge which resist questioning and change. The built-in use of ongoing critical review and evaluation from both within and without the team, use of outside consultants who are not a part of the existent team balance, and changes in personnel and position can contribute toward counteracting this tendency.

The second characteristic is evident in what the public press calls "group think," a phenomenon credited with some of the major blunders in recent national policy. It is an accepted fact of group life that groups exert pressure on their members to conform and that this pressure can inhibit free expression of differences and growth. The team can become merely a rubber stamp when members are unable to criticize, question, and challenge any idea or point of view, regardless of how much or how little support the challenge has among other team members. This tendency toward conformity makes maintenance of the democratic process vital to team life.

In summary, each team is unique, but the process of formation of a vital group unit can be generalized. Equally so, there is wide latitude for variation in composition and structure according to purpose and range of specialization available, but in order to realize the maximum possibilities of the team model, composition and structure must be geared to promotion of the basic democratic process.

Related Readings

Bernstein, Saul (Editor): Explorations in Groupwork. Boston: Boston University School of Social Work, 1965.

Practical and understandable articles on group formation and use. This chapter is particularly indebted to the article by Garland, Jones, and Kolodny on stages of group development.

Beal, George, et al.: Leadership and Dynamic Group Action. Ames, Iowa: Iowa State University Press, 1962.

Consideration of the dynamics of group action and the place of leadership therein.

Brieland, Donald, et al.: The Team Model of Social Work Practice. Syracuse, N.Y.: School of Social Work, 1973.

Series of practical, complementary articles covering the various processes in team formation and operation.

Hare, Paul; Borgotta, Edward; Bates, Robert (Editors): Small Groups; Studies in Interaction. New York: Alfred A. Knopf, 1955.

Well-selected group of articles by a variety of thinkers on various factors in organization and use of small groups.

Horwitz, John: Team Practice and the Specialist. Springfield, Ill.: Charles C. Thomas, 1970.

Excellent small book that reviews research findings and poses the unanswered questions in use of team models.

McGrath, Joseph: Social Psychology; A Brief Introduction. New York: Holt, Rinehart, Winston, 1955.

Good basics in looking at the tasks involved in determining and developing personal relationships within the group.

Northen, Helen: Social Work with Groups. New York: Columbia University Press, 1969.
Good basic text in group formation, dynamics, and the various components that affect use in different settings and for different purposes.
Schwartz, William, and Serapio, R.Z. (Editors): The Practice of Group Work. New York: Columbia University Press, 1971.
Good selection of articles on the use of groups in practice for a variety of purposes. Concepts can be generalized.
Wise, Harold, *et al.*: Making Health Teams Work. Cambridge, Mass.: Ballinger Publishing Company, 1974.
Extremely useful and well-written book about forming and using a team in the health field. Exceptionally good for its consideration of ways of dealing with problems that arise.

CHAPTER 5

THE INTERNAL LIFE OF THE TEAM, II

The effective team possesses unity, cohesion, and solidarity, and its ability to develop these three essential characteristics is strongly related to the manner in which it deals with the value systems and norms of its members and develops ones of its own. As used in this context, "unity" is defined as the oneness of what is varied and diverse; "cohesion," the capacity to retain this unity in the face of both internal and external pressures; and "solidarity," the ability to manifest strength and exert influence as one totality instead of as disparate parts. These terms describe aspects of the wholeness of the team and its capacity to use that wholeness.

Team Values and Norms

Values

"Values" are formulations of standards of worth held by both individuals and groups. They presuppose an evaluation or judgment of that which is "good" or "bad" (*i.e.*, of greater or lesser worth) and rate both goals or wished-for outcomes as well as the behavior seen desirable in moving toward realization of these goals. Values are culturally determined through the process of socialization and the individual use of that process, and while they will always affect behavior, behavior is not always consistent with the values held.

Individuals may not only hold conflicting values within themselves, they also tend to weigh values and modify them by the circumstances surrounding their application. Obviously, people and groups hold conflicting values, and as values usually tend to become internalized and emotion-laden, differences in values can cause conflict that can become intensely personal and difficult to work with.

Norms

While values are formulations of what is worthwhile, "norms" carry an implication of authority. Norms can be defined as those attitudes and behaviors that are expected and/or tolerated of a person in a certain role in a certain group or of a certain group in a certain situation. Norms possess specific characteristics, the understanding of which is vital to effective group functioning. They affect every aspect of team life, in a sense stating "This is the way it is in our team. This is the accepted way our team behaves (works) and the way the members of our team (behave) work."

Norms also have the following characteristics.

1. Norms possess boundaries, which define the range of acceptable behavior. This characteristic lends some flexibility and the capacity to change ways of doing things by deviating from an established pattern to a slightly different one that is still encompassed by the boundaries of the norm. This change, as it is used and accepted, can become the adopted operating norm.

2. Norms are learned. As people enter a new situation, they adapt to the norms of that situation. A new team develops its own norms, and the members participate in the process. New members in a formed team can change norms, but only with acceptance by the team.

3. Norms tend to reflect the setting in which the group exists. For instance, one of the problems that workers in authoritarian settings (such as

correctional institutions) struggle with is maintaining and developing teams and small groups that exercise *democratic* norms of behavior.

4. Norms are enforced by social pressure within the group, and deviations will be subject to question and often rejection by the group. For a variety of reasons, individuals may choose to abide by group norms that do not reflect personal conviction. So long as there is an open, questioning climate in the team, norms are a constructive aspect of team operation, but when they become institutionalized, rigid, and supported by the attitude of "This is the way we've always done things," with the implication that, therefore, there can be no change, norms work to counteract dynamic creativity.

Accommodating Differences

Team members bring their own personal and professional values and norms to the team, and in the process of either building a new team or becoming part of an already formed team, there must be an accommodation among the various norms and values involved. Achievement of this accommodation is a necessary step in team formation, and once it has been achieved, it is a major factor in holding a team together and enabling it to work. It is important to remember that there will be significant differences in values among team members, and this diversity can be a source of strength, in that it promotes a critical attitude and examination of the principles involved.

The three fundamental values, cited earlier, that underlie human services—the worth of human life, the capacity of people for change, and the ability of an outsider to facilitate that change—should be held in common by all team members in human service. Beyond that, there is room for great variation. The manner in which variations are accommodated and the norms that develop will be indicative of the health and strength of the team and whether maximum use can be made of its potential.

The Communication Network

The essential ingredient in working successfully with people individually, in small or large groups, in neighborhoods and communities, in political and geographical areas that cover extensive territory and population, is the ability to establish meaningful communication with them. The difficulties involved in attaining and maintaining clear channels of communication on a one-to-one, face-to-face level are intensified and compounded with the increasing size and heterogeneity of the group involved.

The science and art of interpersonal communication again comprise one of those areas in which a great deal of work is being done, and certain basic principles are emerging that can be used as a starting point in thinking about it.

The Mechanics of Communication

Communication can be defined according to content, as the transfer of meanings, and as a process, whereby through the exchange of messages, a channel is created within which interaction can take place between and among people. The mechanics involved in this process are, on the face of it, relatively simple. A sender or source encodes a message in a way that is designed to convey the intended meaning and sends it along a channel to a receiver, who decodes and receives the message, responds, encodes his response, and returns "feedback." This feedback is at once a "feedforward," in that it carries added elements and moves the process along. This ongoing give-and-take process constitutes communication, but in no sense of the word can it be considered simple, because of the infinite number of variables that contribute to its success or failure.

The conveyance of messages can be put into two categories, verbal and nonverbal. Some writers add a third, the use of symbols, primarily because of their extensive employment as a communication medium in modern society. It is generally estimated that only one third of our messages go through verbal channels; the major part is conveyed on a nonverbal level. Actually, these two media supplement and complement each other, and it is the rare communication that does not employ both. Even a written message carries a nonverbal element in the kind of paper used, the form of printing, the manner of sending. A stiff, heavy, engraved card with "RSVP" at the bottom carries a message apart from the words themselves, and it is different from the symbolic message of a rough sheet of colored mimeographed paper, although both may be invitations to meetings.

It is impossible not to communicate, but it is increasingly possible to learn to understand what we are communicating and how we are communicating it and to control the process in such a way that it can be a consciously purposeful exchange. Initially, this involves considerable self-awareness, because we communicate what we are, and we cannot do otherwise, although we may successfully mislead others at times. Often, because we are not conscious of ourselves, we are genuinely puzzled as to why our efforts to relate with others fail, why our points of view are not heard and accepted, why we incur resentment or hostility or are ignored. It is necessary, therefore, that we know ourselves as well as understand the factors affecting communication as a process.

Learning to Communicate

Communication is a learned process, and as such, it is subject to variation dependent not only on the basic makeup of the communicator but also on his environment, his cultural background, and his socialization. The need to communicate with others is universal, the means by which we survive and develop ways of meeting needs for security, growth, and meaningful relationships. But the manner in which an individual expresses this need, from the moment of the first cry, is shaped and directed by the internal and external pressures to which the individual is subjected throughout his life span. We learn what can be said, to and by whom, under what circumstances, and in what form. But this places on the communicator the burden of being able to perceive realistically who the potential receiver is, what he is thinking and feeling, and what the social situation in which they are communicating requires. Without awareness of these factors and the parts they play, successful communication is impossible.

For example, for many years the predominant form of psychotherapy was based on a psychoanalytic model which required considerable capacity for conceptual thinking and verbalization on the part of the client. Studies of dropouts indicated that many clients exposed to this approach to dealing with personal problems were not accustomed to either thinking or talking about their feelings nor to utilizing concepts. In certain social groups this was actually taboo, and for such people, therapy based on other forms of communication was needed.

Although there is a strong and widespread movement toward more open communication and freer verbalization throughout society, there will always be variations among individuals, based on cultural experience. No one worker can be cognizant of the details and nuances of all these variations, but he can and must learn to be aware of their existence and importance, to respect them, and to recognize, assess, and use cues to their nature available in transactions with other people. Openness to feedback from others and nondefensiveness are essential ingredients in this process.

Communication and Perception

Communication is affected by the manner in which the communicator is perceived, and this perception may be either realistic or distorted. This distortion can arise from feelings, attitudes, previous learning and experiences, or the situation in which the communication is taking place. Usually it is a combination of all these factors. For example, a young mother receiving an Aid to Families of Dependent Children allowance, rendered exceptionally sensitive by her life experience and current situation, was finally able to tell her caseworker how much she resented the arrogance and indifference expressed by the worker's "wearing a mink coat and driving a Cadillac" when she came to visit. The reality was that the supposed mink coat was a well-worn lapin, and the second-hand Cadillac represented the conviction of the worker's husband that this was the best buy in used cars. In this instance, the client was not only getting distorted communication based on misperception, she was also getting two mutually contradictory messages: the verbal one expressive of regard and concern, the nonverbal one expressive of insensitivity and indifference.

In a working situation, when a person in authority is perceived as threatening, communication is frequently distorted, and simple messages dealing with such innocuous issues as policy and procedure may be misread and considered to contain hidden meaning.

The fallibility of perception is exacerbated by a second level of meaning. Communication conveys on one level content and meaning but on a second level carries a message which tells how the receiver is to interpret and use the communication. This second level, known as "metacommunication," arises out of the relationship between the sender and the receiver. It speaks to the relative roles, power and status, feelings and norms of behavior that exist between the two. Specialized relationships, such as student-teacher, parent-child, employee-employer, husband-wife, brother-sister, lend unique meanings to communications that spell out the ways in which they are to be received and used, although the words used in communication may be the same.

In a classroom, for example, one professor might say, "Tomorrow we will discuss Selye's concept of stress," and the student would know that the professor would spend the hour lecturing, and he could safely do nothing but come prepared to take notes. In another class, the metacommunication might say that the student would be expected not only to know who Selye was, but also the specifics of his concept and the pros and cons of the theory, or suffer greatly during class hours.

Group Communication

Communication in a group takes place through the group structure. This factor of group structure affects not only what have been called the "station-to-station" communications—those lacking in feeling and relating only to working roles—but also the "person-to-person" ones—in which work roles are less important, and emotions are more significant. People in a group tend to speak in terms of their roles and what they think their roles require. Those who hold power and status tend to transmit this and to reinforce their own positions by so doing. Those with lesser position do likewise. "Power speaks to power" and lack of power speaks to lack of power, and in such manner subgroups tend to be reinforced. Who speaks, when, how, to what purpose, and to what effect are determined by the way in which the group is structured: sometimes by rigid rules and protocol, sometimes by an unspoken but equally rigid framework of accepted customs and group norms.

In a teachers' meeting, for example, the members of the power structure (principal, assistant principal, and superintendent) would do the talking, teachers would be "invited" to speak at times considered appropriate by the administrators and would be "listened to," but decisions would be made on a high level rather than by consensus and collaboration. In another such group, the discussion might be free and open, informal, and genuinely democratic.

Team Communication

In the initial stages of its development, the team is faced with the task of creating a healthy network of communication among its members. This task is *never* totally completed, throughout the life of the team. If barriers develop, the network will need to be reworked. A part of this effort is the development of a common language of communication, understood and agreed upon by all, not only in terms of the words used and meanings of the nonverbal modes but also of the norms that surround the conveyance of meanings among the members. Once this is established, the newcomer to the team will be faced with the task of learning the team language, learning to encode and decode messages, both open and covert. Until he does so, he will be at a distinct disadvantage in operating in the group.

There is much that can be learned about effective communication, both cognitively and affectively, and a good team experience can foster this learning. Given clarity of purpose and goals; given a climate based on respect for the individual team member, both personally and as a worker, and for the equality and necessity of his contribution; given norms of behavior in communicating that maximize opportunities for openness, receptivity, nondefensiveness, and use of feedback/feedforward to clarify misunderstandings; given committment to the unity of the team, communication patterns can be developed that will not only foster the purpose of the work but also prove a growth experience for the individual members.

Significant team communication is not confined to group meetings. It takes place outside, in individual one-to-one conferences and in small subgroups, and the healthier the climate of team communication and structure, the greater use can be made of these supplementary modes. While it is human nature to gossip and outside discussion of personalities is inevitable, the morale and effectiveness of the team can be destroyed by backbiting and by utilization of these supplementary conferences to express grievances and points of view and attitudes that the possessor does not feel comfortable in bringing out in the team meeting itself. This can be minimized by the creation and maintenance of a "safe" climate in the team, in which these things can be discussed without fear of retaliation.

Earlier, the essential heterogeneity of the human service team was pointed to as one of its strengths in ensuring provision of adequate service. It also can be a source of complication when the specialists are drawn from widely diverse backgrounds and from disciplines which possess languages and communication norms of their own. It can make for development of subgroups along disciplinary lines and increase the chances of misunderstanding across those lines. Such teams will need to make a special effort to accommodate these differences and to ensure maximum openness of climate through conscious use of feedback/feedforward in order to achieve clarification when meanings are not clear.

An Example

A team attempting to deal with basic communication problems exists in the State University Childrens' Diagnostic and Treatment Project, a federally funded program to provide a multidisciplinary approach to work with children and to education of students, specifically in teamwork. Six disciplines are represented: Clinical Psychology, Educational Psychology, Social Work, Speech Pathology, the University Health Services, and the Department of Human Development. In spite of lip service to collaboration, old interdepartmental rivalries and loyalties, as well as personality patterns, created serious difficulties. A major result is the lack of adequate and accepted communication channels, without which the conflicts cannot even begin to be worked on nor the basic roles defined. The resulting climate of discomfort and extreme frustration has resulted in a group of uninvolved team members and frozen students. A teacher invited to present a seminar on principles of communication to all teams reported the following experience.

Prior to the seminar, the teacher requested that questions regarding communication be submitted in advance, in order that she might learn where the major needs of the teams lay, as her conviction was that learning needed to be both didactic and experiential and would be most profitable if there was maximum involvement of participants. The seminar was designed as part of a series, involving all of the students and all six of the supervisors from the various disciplines. Only one of the latter attended. She spent her time reading a newspaper, left in the middle of the meeting, to return in great anger when it ran overtime to say that her schedule was being disrupted.

After a brief presentation of the dynamics of communication, the teacher commented that she had received only one response to her request for input on possible discussion questions. This, obviously, was a breakdown in communication, as no meaningful interchange had resulted. "Can we use this as an example and analyze what is happening?"

In response to this, there was some limited interaction, and the students gradually became somewhat involved. The teacher commented on her own frustration at the lack of participation and her concern as to exactly what the problem was.

Teacher: Is it me, or are students so low on the totem pole in this project that you do not participate in the group discussions and therefore have not learned how to talk about what is going on?

First Student: (hesitating) It's not that we are low on the totem pole . . .

Second Student: Actually, we are told that we are the most important part of the project.

Third Student: We just don't understand what's going on.

Teacher: In what way?

Third Student: We don't understand the technical language the supervisors from the five departments, other than the one where we're placed in, use.

Teacher: Is it impossible for you to speak up in the meeting and simply say that you don't understand and ask for translation into a commonly understood terminology?

(The students exchanged meaningful glances and laughed.)

Fourth Student: (an older woman, with bitterness) We only tried it once. You get cut to pieces and put down as ignorant.

First Student: A couple of the supervisors seem to try, but they just don't seem able to bring it off.

Fourth Student: There always seems to be a hidden agenda at the staffings that comes out through the actual business of the meeting but isn't the business.

In this situation, the students were learning how *not* to be a team. The supervisors had not learned that teamwork requires a surrender of some autonomy in order to achieve greater autonomy as a group. They could not talk to each other or to the students in a meaningful way and therefore could not deal with their own problems of organization and development. The hidden agenda in all meetings, therefore, consisted of the unresolved conflicts, the underground power struggles, the unexpressed angers and frustrations. Such a situation is destructive rather than constructive, and the effect on the participants leaves much to be desired. Such a project requires not only intense personal committment but also common agreement and committment on the part of all of the disciplines involved. In the existent situation, if agreement could be reached on the fact that the project was foundering, employment of an outside consultant might rescue it. Otherwise, it might better disband and start over with new personnel and policies.

Conflict Resolution

The factor of heterogeneity is important not only in communication but also in conflict resolution and decision-making. In addition to the inevitable differences in personalities, there will be differences in values, attitudes, points of view, and ways of thinking and working. Inevitably, conflict will ensue and have to be dealt with. The manner in which the team resolves conflicts and reaches decisions will at once contribute to and be a measure of its effectiveness.

The very word "conflict" is a loaded term; its definition implies increase in physical tension as the individual prepares to deal with a threat—"to fight or to flee"—which carries with it emotional overtones that may be stimulating but not always comfortable. It is viewed variously as destruction, violence, barbarism, loss of control, and irrationality on the one hand; but on the other hand, it can be translated as opportunity, creative impetus, growth, and adventure. The process of individual socialization not only tends to foster this ambivalence of view but also establishes norms as to whether and how conflict shall be permitted, what rules shall be followed, what is fair, and how the outcome shall be decided and dealt with.

One of our major problems in seeing conflict for what it, in reality, is and in using it constructively is our ever-present tendency to think in absolutes, to regard conflict as competition, with the inevitable outcome of winning or losing. This emphasis on the winner/loser syndrome blinds us to the fact that conflict is an essential element, not only in individual lives but in all vital systems, and when constructively used, is one of the most productive forms of collaboration. The sparks from conflict can stimulate creativity, growth, and solutions to problems that appear unresolvable. Those who opt for the "little birds in their nests agree" attitude and sweep elements of conflict out of sight will, at best, be ineffectual and, at worse, actually destructive.

Much work has been done in attempting to understand human conflict, and human service team members would do well to familiarize themselves with this knowledge. We can readily identify three levels around which conflict in such teams usually centers.

First are those conflicts that stem from different and incompatible goals, held by the various persons or groups in the same situation. Goals relate to and arise out of values—those things which are considered of greatest importance and most worth striving for. As pointed out earlier, those values that are of major significance in human service relate to the nature of man and the relationships among men. In origin, they are usually religious, political, or philosophical; they are learned as a part of the socializing process in the family, in peer groups, and in the larger society. Because they tend to become internalized and emotion-laden, the person who differs in what he thinks is important and worth working for is all too frequently perceived as a personal threat and is reacted to as if he were an attacker. In addition, the existence of token values creates problems in this area, when only lip service is given to the basic values of human worth, and the individual is, in reality, operating on the basis of something quite different.

That such conflict arising out of value differences will be a significant factor in team functioning goes without saying. Not only will individual team members hold different values, they may hold the same values but differ in their ideas of how they should be operationalized. If the variations are too great and irreconcilable, it may be impossible for the members to work together, but if there is a basic agreement on the purpose for which the team is founded, the very process of disagreeing about how this purpose should be achieved can be productive. Out of such conflict can come change in policy, purpose, and ways of working.

A second kind of conflict consists of struggles over allocation of goods, rewards, and resources that are either essential or highly valued and exist in limited supply. These can range from the actual material things necessary to sustain life itself, the extras involved in maintaining the standard of living to which we are accustomed which we therefore tend to think are necessary, or power, prestige, or status. All too frequently, individual systems within the larger complex of organizations on all levels tend to approach this allocation wearing blinders, focussing on their own needs and interests. Conflict arising out of such differences can be constructive, in that it requires that systems examine their own needs and wants critically, in light of the needs and wants of others and how they fit into the total pattern. Such conflict can be resolved on a collaborative basis that will strengthen the total overall system, even when this calls for the limitation or phasing out of particular parts.

A third kind of conflict arises when one person or group of persons perceives a threat to his identity and his rights, in either the actions or the existence of another person or group. These tend to be very bitter struggles, indeed, because, in a sense, they are duplications of the primitive struggle for life itself and for meaning of life. In these struggles, reality orientation may be lost, and the opposition may be endowed with qualities of evil that can only be dealt with by total destruction. An atmosphere of mistrust, fear, and hatred may develop that makes constructive use of this kind of conflict difficult. There is a tendency to personalize the situation that not only intensifies the feelings involved but also makes constructive resolution difficult.

Dealing with Conflict

The goal in dealing with conflict is not elimination but *resolution*. Basically, conflict arises from differences, differences between and among people and groups. It is normal, pervasive and can be growth-producing. It can be used as a road to achievement of compromise and collaboration and can strengthen the team. When poorly dealt with, it can destroy a team.

The process of using conflict constructively rests on the following characteristics:

1. Acceptance of the normality of conflict; knowing that it will inevitably exist and that it is understandable, predictable, and manageable.

2. Creation of a climate in which there is freedom to be different, to disagree, and to express feelings about these differences to the extent appropriate in a work situation and to use other resources for dealing with feelings when they are inappropriate; development of group norms that support such a climate is important.

3. Definition of the reality of the conflict, its sources, its boundaries, its possible solutions.

4. Delineation of the small areas of trust and agreement that can be expanded, recognizing that in the height of conflict, these may be difficult to pinpoint; an outsider can be useful here.

5. Consideration on a rational basis, of the various alternatives leading to resolution and use of the team's decision-making apparatus to select and act upon one solution.

Teamwork is not one long battle, but neither is it an exercise in sweetness and light. We know, however, that meaningful relationships among people arise out of shared experiences. A constructive fight is an exercise in use of both the affective and cognitive aspects of the person, and collaboration, the essential ingredient that enables people to work together, is the outcome of the struggle. Once achieved, it is a source of augmented power for the cohesive team, providing strength and energy for the system.

In spite of the fact that conflict is a fundamental ingredient of life, in spite of the fact that democracy as a pattern of government is based on differences and decision-making that results from their resolution, people as individuals frequently have difficulty in using conflict constructively. Workers in human service are no exception.

There is a cultural dimension to fighting, the importance of which is all too often underestimated. People learn to deal with conflict in different ways and without recognition of this and reconciliation of these ways, the team will have trouble getting off the ground in this vital segment of its operation. Learning to present a point of view; to defend that point of view on objective, concrete, rather than emotional, grounds; to confront, if necessary, those who differ, in a constructive rather than a destructive fashion; and to be able to accept and work with the compromise that results from reconciliation of differences may require new learning on the part of the team member.

Each individual team will work out its own way of dealing with conflict and reaching decisions, will develop its own norms and rules for fighting; usually unspoken except when infringed upon. In general, teams tend to stress battling on issues rather than personalities, except when personalities become issues, and to place the personal put-down off limits, except when there are strong bonds and specific norms that make its differential use feasible. Teams vary greatly in the degree and manner of confrontation considered tolerable. In a strong team, fighting can be a source of real satisfaction to the team members and of strength to the team.

Two Examples

Two examples will illustrate ways of using conflict. Scapegoating is a problem in any situation and is doubly serious on a team. The team that permits it is, in a sense, condoning it, and achieving a climate of safety and trust for anyone is thus impossible. When scapegoating is being done by a rank-and-file member, the leader may opt to handle it authoritatively and on an individual basis directly with the offender. In one such reported instance, the leader, who possessed considerable power, merely informed the member that this kind of behavior would not be tolerated under any circumstances.

Unfortunately, people who are scapegoated often invite such reaction in many direct and indirect ways, which almost ensures continuation of this behavior. But if it is recognized and dealt with as the destructive factor it is, chances of repetition will be lessened. When the offender is the leader, the team's problem is more serious, particularly if he has unquestioning support from the overall organization. In such instance, the natural leader or another strong team member can take responsibility for intervening in the situation, either with or without first working on an individual basis with other team members to develop support for such action.

> The new Family Counseling Center had been formed by consolidation of the old County Mental Health Clinic and the old Family Service Association. As is often true in such mergers, the two staffs retained many of their old loyalties, and, as always, there were differences of opinion about location, division of responsibility, choice of executive, etc. These differences and the feelings around them emerged in both the treatment teams and in the general staff meetings. In the latter, they were exacerbated by the conflict between the executive, Les, the former Mental Health Clinic Director, and Randy, the former Family Service Association Director who was now the overall staff supervisor. By virtue of his new power, and partly motivated by underlying personality problems, Les manipulated Randy into the position of being held responsible for all the problems in the new agency. Encouraged by the passivity of the still-divided staff, Les became less temperate and controlled in his behavior.
>
> Finally, an older worker, John, a calm, even-tempered person, respected by all the staff, was disturbed by a particularly destructive meeting and decided something must be done. He sought out two other workers, Mac, from the old Mental Health Clinic Staff, and Sally, recently employed, both of whom had shown indication of strength and ability to work toward internal change. Inviting them out for a beer, he went directly to the point.

> *John:* I was really shook by that scene in staff today, and I'm afraid that if we don't do something about it, we're in for real trouble. Watching your faces, I thought you might share my concern.

Mac: (shaking his head) It sure didn't help things.

Sally: I thought it was horrible. Of course, Randy really asks for it, but Les is getting worse and worse, and the really bad part of it is that none of us does anything—we just sit there.

John: That says something about us as a team, doesn't it?

Sally: It sure does—we're divided and weak. Do you think Les realizes what he is doing?

John: I'm not sure how much of it is conscious and deliberate, but the longer he gets away with it, the worse it's going to get.

Mac: That's for sure. He didn't behave like this in the old clinic days, but this situation with Randy has brought out the worst in him.

Sally: Well, let's do something about it. How shall we start?

Mac: (cautiously) Yeah, he's pretty formidable. He's got the Board in his pocket, and he's a rough infighter with a memory like an elephant.

John: I suspect if we work together, we can handle him. How about. . . .

John's idea was to tackle the problem by demonstrating that Les's behavior was not acceptable to the staff, not by direct confrontation but by unified rejection of it as a way of working. He offered to spearhead this effort, being the most solidly entrenched of the three, and Mac and Sally agreed to support him.

An opportunity to get this plan off the ground was not long in coming. At the next staff meeting, Randy, with considerable nervousness and much hesitation, presented a schedule for coverage of the proposed twenty-four hour walk-in crisis service. Les interrupted him several times with inappropriate comments and finally said, in a heckling voice, "This just won't work at all. You've got all the staff hours conflicting and too much extra time for some of them. With the budget we . . ."

John: (interrupting deliberately and quietly) You know, Les, I don't think Randy's plan is all that bad. There are a couple of places where we might benefit by shifting staff a little, but I'm sure we can be flexible about it. We always have.

Mac: And we're just going to have to plan on a bigger budget if we're going to add this service.

Sally: (chiming in) Randy, maybe I could shift my hours, and instead of the ones I told you I'd take, I could cover Wilma's early shift . . . she's got kids coming home from school, and I don't.

(Wilma, delighted, expresses her appreciation.)

John: (privately thinking that Sally had the Machiavelli touch) Les, has the Board really accepted this whole idea? Are they really behind it? Because it will require more money.

Les, a competent executive, responded to this appropriately, and the staff discussion became general. When in the course of the meeting he returned to attack Randy personally again, the three conspirators intervened, always careful to do so with strongly reality-based support. Randy, encouraged, was able to become less uncertain and less inviting of attack, and the remainder of the staff obviously welcomed the change and went along with it. Afterwards, some commented, with relief, on the good meeting.

This one battle did not win the war, but it was a beginning. Relationships among people are determined in just such small transactions. In spite of his personal problems, Les was sharp enough to get the message—that his staff was beginning to unite and take responsibility for what was happening. It is the rare executive who, unless he is seriously disturbed, does not respond to such pressure. The staff, the other team members, must in turn be aware enough to know what is going on and able to assess its potential for destruction of a team effort and to act together.

This conflict centered around personality problems that were exaggerated by the situation: a merger, with its attendant difficulties, and a staff that could not work as a team.

A second type of conflict, centering around division of limited resources, occurs annually in the Webster County Health Planning Council over budget recommendations, which are made to the County Commissioners. The Council has been in existence for five years and has been blessed with a stable membership, who, by now, know each other well and are used to working together. The Director is a comfortable, easy-going person, who likes and respects variety in people, sets a high standard of performance, and is fair and honest, both in his work and in his assessments of others.

The battle is fought by the five directors of the service systems represented —Webster County Hospital, Garden Heights Nursing Home, the County Welfare Department, Vocational and Rehabilitation Services for the Handicapped, and the Home Health Care Program. It is prepared for months in advance and is fought on the basis of issues. Although five disciplines are represented—medicine, social work, physiotherapy, nursing, and hospital administration—the focus is on the common concern of program planning and financing. These five directors constitute the administrative linkages between the various county systems, with the ultimate responsibility for using constructively the tensions that develop along the interfaces between them.

In the Great Budget Battle, the directors have a dual role, the demands of which sometimes seem contradictory. They represent the interests of their own individual systems, but they also represent the interest of the total overall county program, and somehow these interests have to be reconciled. Whenever possible, final decisions involving continuation, curtailment or expansion of funding are made by consensus, but, if necessary, a vote will determine outcome and final recommendation. In this particular type of conflict, feelings and attitudes are important, as always; disappointments are as keenly felt; and use of power is, as ever, present. It is a pragmatic, well-disciplined, working team in which this is an understood and accepted part of the whole process, a process that is demanding, stimulating, frustrating, but at the same time, satisfying to the participants who enjoy a "good" fight.

Decision-making

The human service team is faced with developing a decision-making apparatus that will not only enable it to deal with itself but, increasingly, will enable it to make significant working decisions for itself and for its host institution. Increasingly in complex organizations, there is a trend toward assigning such responsibility to those who are closest to the problem and therefore, regardless of role and responsibility, possess the primary, relevant information regarding it. There are many different methods used to reach decisions, six of which were identified by Edgar Schein (1969).

1. Decision-making by lack of response is one of the least desirable methods and is a warning signal that the team is in trouble. It indicates withdrawal, nonparticipation, and noninvolvement, for whatever reason, and may imply a lack of committment to decisions that are made in this fashion.
2. Decision-making by authority, wherein the leadership assumes responsibility for deciding on outcome, may be appropriate in terms of an emergency situation or when the decision is primarily administrative, but it is not conducive to maximum development and usage of the strengths of the team model. This criticism in no way implies that use of authority is totally inappropriate. The disciplined and effective worker is able to accept and work with authority: that which accrues to his own operation, that which is a part of the role responsibility of other individuals, and that which is an appropriate part of the team itself.
3. Decision-making by a minority, wherein a small group of decision

makers "railroads" conclusions, is equally undesirable, although frequently practiced. It may signal inappropriate use of power and status, powerlessness or lack of status, or passive noninvolvement of many team members; it also possesses the potential for lack of committment for implementation of decisions in which they take no voice. The team may appropriately allocate responsibility for particular decisions to a specific subgroup, which possesses major expertise in this area.

4. Decision-making by the majority, on the basis of a vote, is probably the most frequently used method, and although purists tend to decry it on the basis that it mitigates against the achievement of maximum collaboration, it provides a necessary shortcut and is frequently the only way in which a decision can be reached. In addition, it is a process to which most people are accustomed and can thus accept. While it may carry unfortunate elements of winning/losing, the ability to fight and lose is essential to operating in a democratic model. This method does not negate the importance of the minority in influencing majority decisions.

5. Decision-making by consensus in which there is prior understanding on the part of all team members that they will accept and abide by decisions of the group even though they have some reservations about them, indicates maturity on the part of the team. It implies recognition of the unity and wholeness of the team and the fact that the members can retain their right to differ and at the same time operate in terms of the totality.

6. Decision-making by unanimous consent, in which all agree, may be a token unanimity when, for a variety of reasons, the team wishes to present a totally united front, or it may represent the actuality of universal agreement. It also represents, for the most part, a high degree of team functioning.

On all teams, there will be those who are decision makers and those who tend to go along. While these tendencies will never be completely overcome, it is a measure of the effectiveness of the teaming when most or all of the members, at best, participate actively in reaching decisions, and, at least, while perhaps not overtly sharing, feel a part of, a responsibility for and a committment to the outcome of the process. It is important that the young team reach a conclusion on how decisions shall be made early in the game, with understanding that, if necessary and desirable, it can be reworked.

It is equally important that the team be committed to the conviction that there are two types of decisions with which it will be involved: those in which the whole team participates appropriately and those which must lie within the purview of a particular specialist or small subgroup of specialists within the team. While familiarity with the reasons for these decisions by individuals or subgroups and openness in discussing them will contribute to team solidarity, respect for judgment based on specialized knowledge is the very essence of teaming. Team members who respect each others' expertise will have no difficulty accepting authority of knowledge. In instances where it is clear and obvious that only the specialist can judge and decide, such as in recommending and implementing a surgical procedure, there is no problem. When valid differences of opinion may exist between team members, such as might arise in a corrections team over whether a delinquent boy should remain at home or be institutionalized, these differences would need to be thrashed out in the team and a decision arrived at, for which both individual and team take responsibility.

It will be easier to do this if we keep in mind that practice in human service is an art based on science and as such requires a margin for error. This should not be used as a facile excuse for work that is less than responsible or for lack of scrupulous evaluation of what is done, but the human service worker must be able to forgive himself and his fellow workers for mistakes. Only if such a climate prevails in the team will members be able to engage in the essential open process of evaluation of what has been and is being done, feel free to make individual decisions based on specialized knowledge, and participate in team decisions.

Related Readings

Boulding, Kenneth: Conflict and Defense: A General Theory. New York: Harper and Row, 1962.
A basic statement of the dynamics of conflict, useful for foundation reading.
Cartwright, Dorian and Zander, Alvin (Editors): Group Dynamics: Research and Theory. New York: Row, Peterson and Company, 1960.
Good collection of articles on group dynamics and the various forces involved therein.
Fast, Julius: Body Language. New York: M. Evans and Company, 1970.
Basic text in an area that is rapidly developing: the use of the body in communication.
Goffman, Erving: Strategic Interaction. Philadelphia: University of Pennsylvania Press, 1961.
Goffman's thesis that communication is based on an assessment of the communicator's thinking is particularly relevant to the team situation.
Hall, Edward: The Silent Language. New York: Fawcett Publications, 1966.

The cultural dimensions of communication, with a usable model for understanding them.

McCrosky, James: An Introduction to Interpersonal Communication. Englewood Cliffs, N.J.: Prentice-Hall, 1971.

Usable and practical introduction to the basis of communication.

Parry, John: The Psychology of Communication. New York: American, 1967.

General theory of communication structure and dynamics.

Rogers, Everett and Shoemaker, Floyd: Communication of Innovation. New York: Free Press, 1971.

Underlying theory and process of the development of communication of new ideas, with the intention of promoting social change.

Schein, Edgar: Process Consultation. Reading, Mass.: Addison-Wesley, 1969.

Practical and useful exposition of the group process.

Schelling, Thomas: The Strategy of Conflict. Cambridge, Mass.: Harvard University Press, 1960.

Basic text in the fundamentals of understanding and using conflict.

CHAPTER 6

THE INTERNAL Life Of THE TEAM, III

The concept of role is one of the most useful tools we have evolved for thinking about people and their relationships with each other. The basic idea has been around for many years, but it was only with the nineteenth century's tremendous burgeoning of interest in scientific examination of man's self and society that we began to understand the complexity of the concept. There is still disagreement about its exact definition. A team can be defined as a system of interlocking roles, and a clear understanding of what is meant by this statement can be most useful for team workers.

Role Definition and Negotiation

For purposes of this discussion, we will combine the ideas of many people and define role as "the sum total of the behaviors expected from a person who occupies a particular position and status in a social pattern." Position is the place occupied in that pattern, and status is the rank or importance *of that place.* This definition rests on certain implicit characteristics of role:

1. Role implies action that is mandatory. It requires that the person in a role behave in a certain way.
2. Role implies transaction with others. The behaviors are carried out in relation with another person or persons; they arise out of social interaction.
3. Role involves perception and expectation: expectation by the actor and those with whom he is interacting of how he should behave, and perception by both as to what the role involves.
4. The behaviors inherent in a role are defined by social norms. Values, judgments, and feelings are involved as to the *right* way the occupant of a particular role *should* behave.
5. Roles tend to demand conformity, although there may exist some leeway for variation within the boundaries. Occupants may be locked into certain expected behaviors by role demands.
6. At any given point in time, people occupy more than one role, and there may be conflict between the expectations and behavior demands of various roles.
7. In any social situation, the role demands placed on an individual may be incompatible with his personal needs, although in work, whenever possible, people tend to go where it looks like these needs will be met and then attempt to play the role in their own way.
8. Changes in role are usually accompanied by stress for the individuals involved.

When an individual becomes part of a team, he will need to learn his role or roles, which will take place through a process of socialization or training for them. He will enter the new situation with certain preconceived expectations based on his perception of the role demands; how he sees it meeting his personal needs; and what his prior experience, both personal and professional, has defined as the norm for behavior in such situations. He will encounter the expectations set down in the definition of his role in the table of organization for the team and those expectations for his behavior of the other team members.

In addition, a new team member enters a social situation that is fluid and in which the role definitions are never finalized. In many instances, as we experiment with different team models and as the team realizes its capacity for growth and self-renewal, roles may be ambiguous, in a state of transition. They may be lacking in certainty and specific definition, as well as in a definite place in the social system that is the team, thus overlapping may exist. They are subject to constant negotiation that is never completely finalized. In order to retain essential team complementarity, there will be constant shifts within all the roles. These changes will require great flexibility on the part of both the team members and the team as a whole, which will, in turn, require constantly evaluating results and making necessary modifications in role requirements.

No matter how specific the definition of role demands, the individual assuming a role will modify it according to his or her own perception of it, personality, and abilities. During the initial shakedown period of the team's existence, these individual variations will become apparent, and the team will move to either accommodate or modify them. When there is a change in individuals who occupy a particular position on the team, the newcomer will be entering a system wherein the role expectations have become set and the balance in the team is dependent on their being performed in a particular way. Accommodation of the new elements in role performance will have to be made and a new balance achieved.

In the literature about modern teamwork in human services, three roles or groups of roles seem to be emerging: the specialist roles, which are defined according to particular knowledge and skill; the leadership roles, which are related to the structure of the team, the requirements of the host institution, and the native endowment of the team members; and a new role or roles which arises out of the need for a single individual on the team to relate to the consumer of the service and integrate with him the total team effort. This latter person, known variously as the team generalist or case manager, relates to the wholeness of the client and frequently provides the essential link of an ongoing relationship that enables the client to make maximum use of the service.

The Generalist Role

The importance of the relationship factor in human services has been apparent since the inception of such service. One of the concerns about the team model is that it not only limits the likelihood of such relationships on the part of the specialists involved but also may limit the effectiveness of the service because of the absence of such ongoing sustaining and enabling contact between a responsible worker and client system: individual, family, or small group. The generalist or case manager role is being designed to provide this essential aspect of service (see Figure 4). Frequently, the various specialists will have limited relationship with the consumer of service, since the boundaries of such relationships are defined by the nature of the particular specialty. The unique element of the generalist's relationship is that it is ongoing and integrative, designed to channel the unified result of the team effort for use of the consumer.

Frequently, this generalist role will be carried by one of the specialists on the team, whose particular expertise qualifies him to assume it in light of the specific problem being dealt with. The generalist role may shift from person to person as the point of intervention into the situation changes, but in view of what we know about the nature of relationship, there is much to be said for retaining ongoing client contact with a single individual from the team.

A significant factor in determining the extent and necessity of this relationship is the capacity of the consumer to utilize the services of the team, and by consumer, we are considering the total gamut of systems which utilize service: individuals, couples, families, small formed groups, neighborhoods, and communities. These systems exist on a continuum that frequently changes during the lifetime of the service. Teaching the consumer to use the services of a body of experts when necessary is itself a part of the service. It is an essential aspect of socialization in our modern, highly complex society, and its absence is a major cause of social breakdown.

The Specialist Role

The comment is frequently encountered in literature on teamwork that the effectiveness of the team is dependent on how clearly the boundaries of the various specialties can be defined and their roles explicated. It is also pointed out that many of the major conflicts between team members arise not out of personality problems but out of lack of role definition or of role definition that is understood and accepted. It seems inevitable that there will be a certain amount of role overlap, except in those instances where the content of the specialty is very specific. This means that role negotiation must be continuous and ongoing, and the effective team creates a climate where this can be maximized and where there is freedom to use unique talents of team members without regard to speciality.

As stated earlier, this need for flexibility in roles can be a source of anxiety for team members whose training has been quite definite

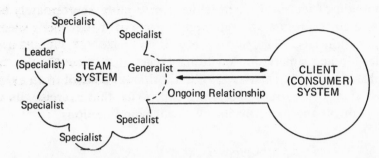

Figure 4. The Developing Role of the Generalist (Coordinator or Case Manager) on Human Service Teams:
(1) Teaches Use of System;
(2) Interprets Actions of System;
(3) Manages Details;
(4) Integrates Totality.

and specific in saying what they can and cannot do, but a team climate that is open to examination of overlap and designation of members on the basis of how the best service can be provided will go far in dealing with this. In a team where there is undue concern with traditional roles, functioning is often poor.

Many teams, particularly those designed to deal with procedures in which emergencies may occur, require that roles be interchangeable, and this whole concept may cause problems for the more conservative role-bound team member. Even in those situations where the worker is generally limited to a defined role, team members are encouraged in the process of orientation to teamwork to learn and practice the other team roles as a way of increasing understanding of and ability to work with each other, as well as to deal with emergencies in particular situations.

In the cardiac catherization team of the Pediatric Section of Bowman Hospital, for example, this interchangeability of roles is stressed. Team members include two physicians, a nurse, and two technicians, any one of whom is able to perform the other team roles in an emergency situation. This kind of flexibility requires not only understanding of other roles but also respect for them and their requirements.

The Leadership Role

The role of the leader on a team is subject to considerable scrutiny in the various developing models. Frequently, supervision is considered a function of leadership, and while it may quite appropriately be so considered, there are some unique aspects of it that merit separate examination (see "The Supervisory Role," page 92). Present use of leadership and supervision on teams ranges along a continuum, from emphasis on a particular type of authoritarian control to an existentialist type of unstructured group experience that exercises its own peer controls and performs its own leadership functions.

Leadership for Optimal Team Functioning

Researchers have been enquiring for many years into various kinds of leadership, seeking answers to the question of what model is most effective in enabling people to do their best work and thus produce the best results. Out of this research have come some general findings:

1. People who are seriously and maturely involved in their work situations, who have a committment to achievement of the overall purpose for which these situations are devised desire and respect structure and stability, order in working procedures, efficiency, and good administration and are willing and able to accept and delegate authority for this purpose.

2. People work best when stress on status and hierarchy is minimal and when the relationships among workers on all levels are collegial rather than hierarchical. (By definition, "collegial" is used to mean relationships based on respect for individual integrity, knowledge, and skill and recognition of their value and the value of the persons exercising them. "Hierarchical" is used in the sense of meaning dictatorial control based on status and position, lacking in recognition of the worth and integrity of the individual, both as a person and as a worker.)

3. People work most effectively, creatively, and happily and are able to use their abilities to the greatest extent in those groups where controls are neither autocratic nor laissez-faire but based on sound democratic principles. (These particular findings tend to substantiate the principle that people have both a basic need and a right to be involved in decision-making in matters pertaining to their own welfare.)

4. People work best in a humane work situation, which provides a structure flexible enough to accommodate individual needs, not only in terms of such aspects as autonomy, the sharing of information, participating in the making of decisions, and provision for dealing with grievances but also in everyday details, such as working hours, time off, and physical surroundings.

5. People work best in those situations where there is a clearly defined

expectation in regard to level of performance, based on awareness that knowledge and skills cannot be mandated or defined by rules and regulations.

6. People are interested in learning and acquiring new working skills but tend to resist the teaching of them, as they require an accommodation that may be difficult and sometimes painful.

7. People work best in a situation where fairness is practised in the sense of equal reward for equal performance and a minimal use of special privilege, particularly unearned.

Within the framework of these findings, the team and the organization need to provide for forms of leadership and supervision, wherein the authority inherent in performance of these two roles will be used to perform the following functions:

1. The managing or arranging of functions, involving: the provision of physical space and equipment, budgeting, and organization of both people and things in an orderly fashion.

2. The liason functions with the host institution, which may involve arranging for resources, working out policies and problems, interpreting the work of the team, fitting the team into the total system.

3. Chair functions in team meetings, including: providing the essentials, without which meetings founder, such as providing resources, setting time and place, sending out notices, securing equipment; providing facts, keeping the discussion focussed and moving, being prepared to clarify, summarize, stress certain points, support when necessary; helping create an informal, cooperative, permissive, and enabling climate; providing necessary followup on discussions and decisions.

4. Assessing and evaluating the work done, the worker, and the progress of the team, particularly in light of the team's overall purpose and that of the host institution in which it operates. Out of this should come recommendations for retention and continuation of personnel, promotions, raises, salaries.

5. Informing, teaching, and consulting with regard to both the work of the team and the work of the individual specialists.

Not all of these functions are actually performed by the team member who is leader or supervisor, but responsibility for them rests with persons in those positions. The functions themselves may be designated to others.

Types of Team Leadership

At present, team leadership seems to fall into one of three categories or some combination of the three: designated, emergent, and situational.

The designated leader is selected by the host organization or by the team itself to perform the leadership role. His responsibilities are usually clearly and specifically defined. He may simultaneously occupy the role of one of the team specialists, or he may be purely administrative in function. This latter aspect may determine where he "sits" in relation to the other team members. If he is both specialist and administrative leader, he may find that the role requirements involved in collegial specialization and administrative authority conflict.

Almost every team has a "natural" leader or leaders, who are here classified as emergent, because they usually arise in the process of team operation. It is not at all uncommon to find both designated and emergent leadership, but if both are present, their smooth collaborative functioning is vital to team performance. When there is ongoing conflict between the two, the team is often split by dissension. Frequently, the emergent leader fills the essential role of acting as a focus for dissatisfaction with designated leadership and as an enabler of efforts to change. The emergent leader is one of the team specialists, a collegial member of the team, and may arise from any position or status. Personal charisma, authority of knowledge, ability to use the system in which the team operates with maximum effectiveness, ability to communicate effectively and to work with diverse people comfortably are usually at the basis of this emergent capacity for leadership. The emergent leader may become the designated leader because of these very characteristics.

Finally, team models increasingly make use of what is known as situational leadership, in which the leader changes with the situation. The team member possessing the greatest skill and knowledge in the particular work area with which the team is currently engaged will provide leadership in that particular effort. This is a very specialized kind of leadership and does not encompass the total range of functions, for which continuous and ongoing responsibility is needed, such as provision of resources, arranging, and maintenance, but it has a legitimate place in teamwork and is increasingly used as the team matures and is able to make use of the fullest capacities of all of its members.

Effective team members can accept and work with the fact that the leadership role will move from person to person according to the kind of expertise that is used to deal with a particular matter under consideration. Initially, this may pose a problem for the team member unaccustomed to exercising this kind of authority of knowledge, as well as for the member whose education and status have prepared him to assume the leadership role in all circumstances. In order to use its members' skills to greatest advantage, the team will need to ensure that this role can move freely and appropriately from person to person.

An Example of Team Leadership

Lakewood Diagnostic Center adopted a team approach to work on its adolescent service, with teams including psychiatrist, psychologist, social worker, nurse, recreational therapist, and ward aide. Each team designated its own formal leader, and in the instance of Team B, the psychologist was selected for this role, in part on the basis of her previous experience in using the team structure in another hospital. Initially, she scheduled a two-hour morning meeting in order to get acquainted, define roles, and provide opportunity for members to begin to engage themselves with the team structure and familiarize themselves with all the roles. In addition, the meeting served to define the team purpose, in accordance with the overall purpose of the institution, as study, diagnosis, and implementation of a treatment plan. It was agreed that both individual and group modalities were to be used to achieve this and to make the mandatory sixty-day hospitalization a constructive living experience for the young person.

The psychiatrist's role was defined as responsibility for all drug therapy; for direct provision of medical care or for securing consultation from other medical specialists; for participation in diagnostic study and in psychotherapy.

The psychologist, in addition to being the designated team leader, with all that this involved in terms of planning and directing, administered various psychological tests and was responsible for implementing and directing programs utilizing behavior modification techniques differentially with various patients in order to facilitate adaptation and maximum usage of the institutional experience.

The nurse and the ward aide were intimately involved in the ongoing life space of the adolescents and formed a small team in themselves by virtue of their unique roles. The nurse was responsible for the organization of the structure of ward life, administration of medication and necessary nursing care, and supervision of the aides and licensed practical nurses on the ward. The aide, a young part-time student, actively participated in the ongoing life of the ward and in formal and informal individual and group discussions and accompanied the patients on special outings.

The recreational therapist's role involved her with the adolescents both on and off the ward in various recreation programs, as well as in evaluating and contributing to the diagnostic study and the treatment plan.

Finally, the social worker functioned as the liason with the family and the community, contributed a social study, and became particularly active in predischarge plans and follow-up as necessary.

Obviously there were varied levels of both experiential and theoretical knowledge represented in this team, as well as levels of skill in performing varied functions. The time spent in careful and specific role definition paid off, as did the designated leader's orientation to a flexible concept of leadership, wherein the aide learned to be comfortable in assuming an authoritative stance when the major concern under consideration was the kind of relationship he was able to develop and maintain with the patients. Team members learned to be open to questions regarding what they were doing and why. Probably the area of most difference, in which most discussion was needed, was use of behavior modification to affect life-style. As this involved all team members in their contacts with the adolescents, it required unanimity of committment and action, which develops only when based on clear understanding and acceptance. The psychologist's role in this area involved teaching and supervision.

On this team, the members learned from each other because of their openness to this kind of learning, their acknowledgment of varying expertise, and their acceptance of the shift in leadership role with the shift in the work being done.

The Supervisory Role

It is obvious to even the most casual observer that there are special factors that must be taken into consideration in providing useful supervision for teams. They have to do with the nature of the team itself, the basis of differentiation for the specializations involved, and the capacity of the individual worker for autonomous practice.

There are two kinds of teams currently evolving in human service.

The first, which we can designate the "intradisciplinary" team, is made up of people whose orientation is to one discipline but who represent differing aspects of that discipline and differing educational levels and who perform differing roles. This model is being widely used in teaching and social work at the present time. The teaching team might include the school principal, the classroom teacher, the teacher's aide (who is often a student in a teaching program), and the parental aide. In social work, the team in a family counseling agency could consist of the director (who possesses a doctoral degree), the supervisor (with a master's degree), the caseworker (with a bachelor's degree), the technician in human services (who is a graduate of a two-year community college program), and an indigenous worker.

The team members not only operate from the same basis of theoretical knowledge but also use many of the same skills, with some variations in technique. The basis for differentiation lies in the varying levels of academic and experiential learning, in varying responsibilities, and in varying rewards. A major problem with these teams is overlap and unclear designation of role responsibilities. If responsibility for supervisory functions is clearly defined, providing role definitions should be no problem, as there is a common knowledge base, but it must be very clear as to who does what, who supervises who, and what preparation is needed for that particular role.

The second major model is that of the "interdisciplinary" team, whose specialists are drawn from many different disciplines, the content of whose specialized knowledge and skills is unique to that particular individual occupying that particular position. When content of knowledge is so highly specialized, it is difficult, if not impossible, to find a person who can provide the evaluating and teaching functions of supervision for all these practitioners. Such teams are frequently seen in comprehensive care centers, where such differing specialists as a chemist, a geneticist, a psychologist, a social worker, and a family planning specialist could be involved. To make the picture even more complicated, these teams could include workers drawn from varying educational levels within these disciplines.

Related to this is the whole question of the capacity of the specialist for autonomous or independent and self-governing practice. The older professions, such as medicine and law, certify that their graduates are prepared for this. Most professions consider holders of their terminal degree as so qualified, but it is increasingly accepted that in human service, there exist many jobs for which this kind of preparation is neither necessary nor desirable. By definition, the team member should be capable of a degree of autonomous practice in filling the role for which he is employed. In part, his specialized ability fits him for the role, but continued teaching and learning are essential, and provision for them needs to be built into the team model, not only in the content of the various specializations but also in the process of teaming.

Increasingly, the teaching and learning functions of supervision in modern human service teams are being performed by the team itself, through use of outside consultants and by workshops, seminars, and other group learning devices. These are used to complement and supplement each other. Impetus and planning for them may originate with the team itself or with the host institution and its administrative staff.

Peer Supervision

Peer supervision demands not only a high level of maturity and responsibility on the part of the team members for both performance and outcome, it also depends on the existence of an open and secure team climate, in which, while it may be uncomfortable, it is safe and generally rewarding to bring up concerns and participate in discussion regarding others as well as oneself. Capacity to participate in and use peer supervision is based not only on knowledge of the team process but also on awareness of what the various roles involve and on respect for fellow team members, both as persons and as practitioners. For this reason, team workers frequently make an effort to observe and learn something about the other jobs on the team. Thus, the social worker assigned to a rural health team might spend some time assisting the physician with home deliveries, helping the nurse do school checkups, aiding the lab technicians. In turn, he might actively involve these other specialists in aspects of his role: social planning with an aged client, counseling a young unmarried mother, helping the family of an adolescent delinquent.

Peer supervision also places very special demands on the administrative representative on the team, whose power is real and can easily be misused or perceived as being misused. As a participant in this process, the administrator needs to speak with the authority of knowledge and to minimize his position in the administrative structure in order to facilitate development of an open climate, which fosters maximum objectivity of evaluation. It also requires that the other high status members of the team, whose professional orientation frequently places them in the role of decision makers for others and fosters development of the attitude that their knowledge equips them to be equally knowledgeable in all fields, strive to achieve the openness that will enable them to hear and use the comments of their fellows.

Responsibility for Team Leadership/Supervision

A democratic organization, by its very nature, is responsible for its own functioning and, as such, modern human service teams need to develop their own leadership and supervision. Exercise of these processes can go far in limiting development of hierarchies and a closing bureaucratic system. This does not mean, however, that there are no problems inherent in this process. Not only does it require a high degree of maturity, it also requires a sense of group responsibility, which should develop as the team evolves. It is necessary to recognize that that which is everyone's responsibility frequently becomes no one's responsibility and to keep in mind that there must be built-in provisions for monitoring the work of the team if it is truly accountable for what it does both to its host organization and to the total society.

In addition, if it is a team that by necessity involves close relationships, discussion of personal and social characteristics may be necessary. While this can raise an issue of the right to privacy and confidentiality, in general individuals feel freer to discuss matters in groups. We have learned that it is often beneficial rather than harmful to do so; that in any organization, confidentiality is usually an academic concept, lacking in real substance (most people generally have a pretty good idea of what is going on); that by making a fetish of confidentiality, we are often implying that that which cannot be discussed is so degrading it must be kept under cover; and finally, that confidentiality often implies that those persons to whom information must be denied cannot be trusted to use it wisely. Perhaps in this, as in so many other questions, there is no absolute. The individual should have a voice in deciding what can be discussed on the team, and other discussion options should be open for consideration, such as individual conferences.

The team that undertakes responsibility for its own leadership and supervision must be prepared to deal with: (1) the competitiveness of its members; (2) the fact that individuals can hide in a group; (3) the need for support and even rescuing of individual members, at times; (4) the tendency of groups to scapegoat; (5) the tendency of groups to seek a bland and comfortable level of functioning rather than openly face and resolve differences.

On the positive side, group leadership and supervision can provide real opportunity and stimulation for learning and for the development of responsibility through exercising responsibility. In this process, communication is mandatory and tends to improve, both within the team meetings and in the increasingly frequent between-member conferences which accompany use of this model. As the team shares responsibility for total outcome, factionalism and defensiveness are lessened, and morale tends to improve.

Power, Position, and Status

Power

The reality of power is a factor that anyone working in human service must be prepared to deal with, and nowhere to a greater extent than in the team model of practice. The person or group possessing power possesses it in relation to another person or persons. There is no power without someone to be powerful over. It is ubiquitous, always present, and because of the social aspects of team membership, particularly significant, not only in understanding what is happening in the team but in working with it. All too often, power is regarded as a loaded term, with an unpleasant connotation that has led to its being ignored rather than studied and used consciously and constructively. Actually, power in and of itself is neither good nor bad. It is an inescapable reality, which can be used toward achievement of constructive or destructive ends.

Sources of Power

The dictionary definition of power is "the ability to act." To this, for our purposes, we might add "in relation to others." Power can be exercised by an individual or by a social system and is generally seen as deriving from five sources:

1. The ability to punish or coerce. (Physical coercion is considered the ultimate source of power, but there are many other ways in which this kind of power can be exercised, such as the withholding of raises and promotions and assignment to low positions.)

2. The ability to reward, on the other end of the continuum from the first source. (Power can reward with recognition, promotions, raises, and assignment to high positions.)

3. The ability to know, which comes from knowledge, skill, and expertness.

4. The ability to exercise the legitimate authority inherent in a position, such as that of a designated leader or director.

5. The ability to exercise influence through allocation of resources, both people and things, such as that which is exercised by the nondesignated leaders in a community, who, by virtue of who and what they know and control, may hold the actual power within the system.

6. The ability to exercise referent power, which derives from expectations that accompany a certain role to which other people defer. An example is the physician on a committee, to whom people give power because of their own attitudes towards his role.

Power is a continuous factor in the life of the person, from birth to death. The manner in which he is able to cope with it is closely related to his developmental experiences and his learned pattern of living. Powerlessness can be a source of anxiety and insecurity and contribute to a low self-image. It tends to reinforce itself, and the group member who feels that he is without power will have trouble operating as a full and contributing member of a democratically structured team.

Use of Power

We can think of the power structure in a team as existing on two levels: the formal and the informal. The formal power structure consists of those persons who, by virtue of their designated positions, status, and roles, possess power to control, punish, or reward; the informal power holders are those who possess power by virtue of their capacity for natural leadership, referent qualities, knowledge, etc. The structure that evolves around these two power patterns will affect all vital team operations. Norms will center around it. The communications network will be affected, in that people with power tend to talk to other people with power, information being withheld or shared according to their decisions; communication thus assumes significance when imparted by them; they tend to talk down to the powerless, who, in turn, talk up to the powerful. Working patterns, assignment of tasks, decision-making, all are affected by who has what power and how it is used.

The team, therefore, must learn what and where the power is, both within itself and within the organization of which it is a part. It must very consciously develop its own power structure in such a way that it will contribute to maximum effectiveness and constructive use of its personnel. Vital to this is the creation of a "safe" climate, in which the traditionally powerless are able to differ without fear of retaliation. The team must learn what unique power is possessed by individual team members and by the team itself that can be put to use to achieve the purpose of the team. When it is faced with the problem of internal or external power that is destructive to individuals, to the team, or to its work, the team must identify its source and develop a strategy to cope with it.

Useful in this latter undertaking is the fact that power is a dynamic, constantly changing force and that it is possessed of a "delicate balance," with a trend toward imbalance. This imbalance creates a reciprocity that can be used. In dealing with power, it is necessary to identify the sources of latent power that exist and to form new coalitions or power structures that will implement these sources.

One of the most interesting examples of this within the past decade in human service is the development and use of the latent power that exists within client or consumer groups, which have formed effective coalitions in many areas and have learned how to use existent power. One of the most powerful of such groups is represented by the parents of retarded children, who have been able to influence legislation and change the whole pattern of services to the retarded.

A most difficult problem in this area and, sadly, one that is seen frequently is the presence on a team of a powerful person or persons, often supported by the organization, who use their power over the people of lesser status and position to manipulate, to enforce their own will, and to subvert the democratic process of the team. Team members who are lower on the totem pole may be reluctant or actually frightened to tackle these people, but as they affect the work of the team, they must be faced. In such instances, the creation of a crisis that will lead to demonstration of the fact that the team work is suffering may be useful in precipitating necessary change. Employment of an outside consultant to provide objective evaluation of what is happening and facilitate reorganization can also be useful.

Power in the team model should be used in a manner consistent with democratic principles. It exists on three different levels: the power of the total team, which is a part of its gestalt; the power of groups within the team; and the power of individuals within the team. The possession of power is related to position and status, although power does not inevitably go with position.

Position

Position is the place the team member occupies in the pattern of team life, and it relates to the function the team member performs. For example, the team leader occupies a position for which certain functions are prescribed: planning, organizing, etc. As a leader, he also has certain status or relative rank in relation to the other team members, and the rights and responsibilities that accrue to that status in that particular team are automatically his.

It is important to keep in mind that teams may differ in the status accorded to various positions, as well as in the way that status and the power implicit in it are used. For example, on one team, the designated leader may possess and use the attributes that traditionally accompany that position and status—access to information and resources, psychological strength—to determine the direction and operation of the team. On another team, he may possess the position and status, but the actual power lies in the hands of a so-called "natural" leader, who, by virtue of personal characteristics and qualifications, is accorded that power by the team and uses it accordingly. Position and status are essential parts of team structure, as they constitute the way the work is divided and the diverse functions organized.

Status

In any group, there tend to be three status levels, the upper, the middle, and the lower, and there is a strong tendency toward the formation of subgroups along the lines of these three levels. Teams are no exception to this, although the smaller the group, the less likelihood there is that subgroup alignment will take place. If it does develop and assume real rigidity, it can work against the development of the team into an effective unit which uses the abilities of all of its members to greatest advantage. Power generally lies with the upper or "elite" group of members, who tend to direct and control by various means those below them. It is pretty well substantiated by research findings that the middle group usually aligns itself with the elite group, leaving those in the lower group without allies and with even less power. Competition may develop for admission to the elite group, with adverse effect on the unity of the team.

Modern teams are naturally susceptible to development of these three status groups. Members represent many and varying levels of social and professional or nonprofessional status, are assigned different roles that carry status, are rewarded differently for their work. Friendship groups tend to develop because of commonality of interests, and there is carry-over into the work situation.

Integration with Team Values and Norms

In Chapter 5, it was pointed out that as a part of its developmental process, the team evolves its own value system and supporting norms. Position, status, and power and their use are subject to the controls inherent in these values and norms. It is important, therefore, that the team evolve a base of values and norms that enables it to use all its members to maximum advantage. For example, access to information and participation in decision-making are fundamentals of team practice. The strongly democratic team operates from a value and norm base that says, "On our team, all information is shared fully and freely by everyone, and decisions are reached through a process of discussion and consensus." Another team might operate from the base of, "On our team, only the elite group has access to crucial information and only its members participate in decision-making."

The purpose of the team, the extent to which the various members are capable of participation on the basis of individual expertise, and the role demands of the positions they hold would determine where members stand in relation to the various aspects of team operation. If the team climate is democratic in the sense of valuing the unique contribution of each member, it will much more likely be able to constructively use power in all of its various aspects.

The problems inherent in improper use of power on a team can be exacerbated if there exists a discrepancy between the outward organization of the team and the covert organization—between what it says it does and what it actually does—in terms of respecting the differences among team members. This can be much more demoralizing and destructive to team operation than even the development of rigid hierarchies that constrain individual members or groups.

The effective team, then, must:

1. Recognize the reality of power, understand and accept it, and be prepared to use it.
2. Know where power is, who possesses it, why it is there, and how it is being exercised.
3. Evaluate its use in light of whether it contributes to the particular kind of team operation needed to realize the unique purpose of the team.
4. Know how it can be changed if it is destructive or not fulfilling a constructive purpose.

Entrenched power is very difficult to change. It is much easier if the new team can develop the necessary base of values and norms, which will promote constructive use of power, but it is the rare team that does not have to struggle at some point with this problem. As pointed out earlier, the fact that power has an equilibrium is an asset when change is desired. The balance of power can be upset and reorganization triggered by changes in policy, personnel, and input.

The fundamental changes taking place in a society and in the definition and role of human service within that society are currently promoting extensive challenging of entrenched power. At present, we in human service are in the process of examining and experimenting to determine how desired changes in existent systems can be brought about.

Related Readings

Barker, Robert and Briggs, Thomas: Using Teams to Deliver Social Services. Syracuse: Syracuse University Press, 1969.
Emphasis on utilization of manpower in human services, on the basis of where the worker can perform most effectively.
Flippo, Edwin B.: Principles of Personnel Management. New York: McGraw-Hill, 1971.
Basic principles and review of processes in selecting and managing personnel.

Gross, Neal *et al.*: Explorations in Role Analysis. New York: John Wiley, 1958.
Basic text useful in contributing to understanding of what is involved in the concept of social role, in its various components.

Kahn, Robert *et al.*: Organizational Stress—Studies in Role Conflict and Ambiguity. New York: John Wiley, 1964.
Variety of presentations on the effect of problems in role designation and clarity on job performance.

Klein, Allan: Effective Groupwork. New York: Association Press, 1972.
Comprehensive and well-written text on use of groups in practice. Refer also to Role Playing in Leadership Training and Group Problem Solving, published in 1956 by this same author. Principles broadly applicable.

Mills, Theodore: The Sociology of Small Groups. Englewood Cliffs, N.J.: Prentice-Hall, 1967.
Emphasis on the group as a unit and on the forces that hold it together.

Perlman, Helen: Persona, Social Role and Responsibility. Chicago: University of Chicago Press, 1968.
One of the best for readability, usability, and validity and in understanding the concept of social role.

Stein, Herman and Cloward, Richard (Editors): Social Perspectives on Behavior. Glencoe, Ill.: Free Press, 1958.
Among other useful things, good section on social role in its various aspects.

Thomas, Edwin (Editor): Behavioral Science for Social Workers. Englewood Cliffs, N.J.: Prentice-Hall, 1967.
Good collection of articles on application of theory to practice.

CHAPTER 7

The External life of the team

A team does not operate in a vacuum. It is both a total system within itself and a component of larger systems. As such, its second major responsibility (after dealing with itself) lies in dealing with a triple set of environmental relationships: (1) relationships with the other subsystems within the host organization; (2) relationships with the organization itself; and (3) relationships with the overall community. This triple responsibility leads to an exceedingly "complex set of give-and-take relationships," the nature, intensity, and demands of which depend on the situation of the team, its basic purpose, and the part it is designed to play in the overall picture. The definition, establishment, and maintenance of these relationships constitute an essential part of the team's work.

The Team and the Host Organization

Organizations in human service are growing increasingly larger and more complex, and it is in large organizations that offer a wide variety of diverse services that teams are most frequently found. Knowledge of how the organizations, as wholes, function is crucial to the success of the teams within them.

For many years, organizations were conceptualized in terms of the classic pyramid. At the top was the boss and immediately below him, the straw bosses. At the bottom were the workers, each considered as an individual. Direction and decision-making were executed at the top of the pyramid, and knowledge and energy flowed downward to the workers, with very little give-and-take or sharing of responsibility for the total organization along the way. Figure 5 illustrates this setup with the simple structure of a poor relief society in 1900, which operated both a woodyard and a depot for the distribution of used clothing and household goods. The director "directed" the total organization. Under him were two assistants: one to "run" the woodyard, one to "run" the clothing depot. The workers related to the director and his assistants as those who "told them what to do," the assistants relaying the bosses' orders. It is interesting, in terms of the concept of human relationships that

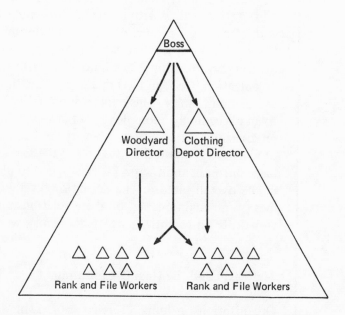

Figure 5. Patterns of Organization: I, Poor Relief Society, 1900

prevailed at this time, that the director of poor relief in one city was known as the "Poormaster."

Then organizations began to grow in size and complexity. Philosophically, the earlier simplistic view of man was abandoned as knowledge of his complexity, variability, and multitudinous needs increased. A new concept of power, based on collaboration and reason rather than fear and coercion, developed, and organizational values began to shift from depersonalized, mechanized ones to more humanized, democratic ones. The concept of the responsibility of the workers for the whole of which they were a part changed and enlarged. As knowledge and skills became highly specialized, groups of workers focussing on one particular aspect of the work became necessary, and the pyramidal structure no longer sufficed to describe what existed in an organization. Modern organizations have evolved into a cluster of interacting and interrelating systems, and the modern team in human service is only one aspect of the whole.

Except for the individual person—who can be thought of as a highly specialized system—the team is the smallest systems unit within the organization. In the opinion of some theoreticians, systems within an organization should not be regarded as subsystems but as discrete systems operating in relation to each other. This conviction is based on the size and relative autonomy of some systems. But regardless of these factors, the basic principles of relationships are the same, and they would seem to be better described by use of the concept of subsystems, each existing as part of a larger whole.

Subsystems in a Modern Organization

Figures 6 and 7 illustrate what has happened and is happening to patterns of organization in human service. Figure 6 represents a modern family service agency, which operates three divisions: a family counseling service, an adoption and foster care program, and a day care center. This agency utilizes a team model of operation and is organized into four working teams. Overall planning and administrative responsibilities are carried out by a team made up of the director and three supervisors, who are designated in the organizational chart of the agency, whose roles are defined, and whose expertise in this area is specified as a condition of employment. The supervisors provide the liaison between the service teams and the

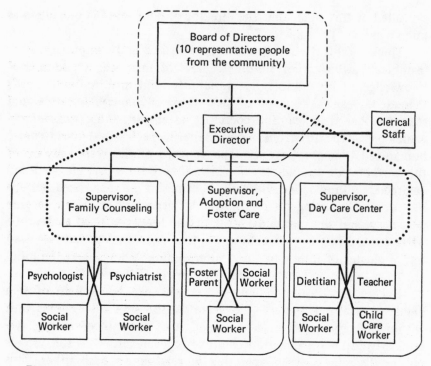

Figure 6. Patterns of Organization: II, A Modern Family Service Agency
The Systems:
— — — Policy-Making and Community Linkage
•••••••• Planning and Administration
————— Service Delivery

administration, and at present, there is some consideration of having a rank-and-file worker from each of the service teams and a representative of the client group work as a part of the administrative team. Even without this, there is a fairly free and open give-and-take between these four subsystems.

Each of the three divisions operates as a team, with regular meetings and shared responsibility for the work. Team I, in the Family Counseling division, consists of the supervisor, who is a psychologist, two social workers, and a minister, who specializes in pastoral counseling. Team II, in the Adoption and Foster Care division, consists of the supervisor, who is a social worker, two other social workers, and two foster parents. Team III, in the Day Care division, consists of the supervisor, who is a teacher, a social worker, a dietitian, several day care workers, two aides, and two parents.

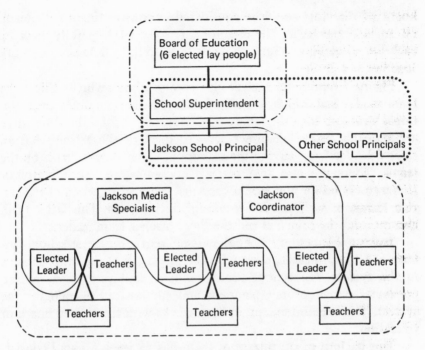

Figure 7. Patterns of Organization: III, Jackson Elementary School
The Systems:
—·—·— Policy-Making and Community Liaison
·········· Total System Planning and Administration
————— Jackson School Planning and Administration
————— Service Delivery

Each of these teams employs various specialists as consultants from time to time, such as a psychiatrist, a pediatrician, and a public welfare worker. Each team is responsible for operating its own program, for utilizing the specialized knowledge and skills of its members, and for relating to the other teams that are subsystems within the organization and to the organization itself—receiving input from them and returning output to them. Each team also relates to the community in which it operates, both directly through its services to clients and its contact with other community resources and indirectly through the executive director and the board of directors of its sponsoring organization.

This being an agency supported by a combination of private donations and federal tax funds and sanctioned by the community through interested lay people, the director of the agency and the board of directors could be considered as constituting a fifth team, on an informal basis. The directors are selected, hopefully, because each has something unique to contribute to the whole and can work together as a group.

Figure 7 represents a small elementary school, which utilizes the team model and which is part of an even more complex organizational structure than the family service agency. Again, there are three major teams providing direct service. Each of these teams has an elected leader from among the classroom teachers who make up the teams. There are also two special services people, coordinator or guidance counselor and media specialist, who serve on all of the service teams, as well as on the administrative team. This latter team also includes the principal and the three teacher team leaders.

Jackson Elementary School is itself part of a larger school system, and the principal serves with the principals of the other schools in the system, the school superintendent, and various specialized personnel on an overall planning and administrative team for the system. The superintendent, in turn, works with the elected board of education.

This pattern of organization, then, has six levels. Team I consists of the kindergarten and first and second grade classroom teachers, the coordinator, and the media specialist. Team II consists of the third and fourth grade classroom teachers, the coordinator, and the media specialist. Team III consists of the fifth and sixth grade classroom teachers, the coordinator, and the media specialist. These three teams plan and put into operation the curriculum for their respective areas and consider the special needs of the students and their families and ways to meet them.

Team IV consists of the principal, the elected leaders of the three service teams, and the two special services people. Its purpose is to plan and provide for the maintenance needs of the teams, to coordinate their operations, and to set and carry out administrative policy within the school district. Team V consists of the school superintendent, various specialized personnel, and the principals of all the schools in the system. Its purpose is to provide administrative services for the total school system. There is yet another level above this, the elected board of education, which provides the first line of relationships with the total community and which is the policy-setting body for the total system.

Levels of Organization

The two modern human service organizations presented here are relatively simple, and for purposes of illustration, only a skeleton sample of the people actually involved in the organizations are cited. Many organizations are too complex to present diagramatically. A modern, comprehensive health care center, such as those which have developed around the great hospitals and which, because of the necessary variety and specialization of disciplines represented, predominantly use the team model of service delivery, are good examples of this.

The introduction of federal planning and funding have added an even vaster dimension to the already complicated pattern of local and state systems. It is the rare human service program that is not involved in some way on a national level, and this requires the development and maintenance of a whole different constellation of relationships.

The multiplicity of these inter- and intra-system relationships in such an organization is almost overwhelming, and yet clarity and understanding about them is essential to working with them. For this reason, it is imperative that the team worker comprehend the characteristics and basic principles of operation and organization in systems, in general.

Understanding Systems

Keeping in mind that systems theory is a tool for thinking and understanding, we can begin by defining a system as a whole made up of interrelated parts. In addition, all vital systems must meet two requirements, they must provide for maintenance of the status quo and for growth. At first glance, these requirements might seem to be mutually exclusive, but in actuality, they complement and supplement each other. By their very nature, systems, as they grow older, have a tendency to use more and more of their energy just to maintain themselves. They have learned the ways to operate that work for them, so they develop a tendency to continue to use these ways and to become "closed" to the input that might require that they change. Just as older people, older systems have a tendency to become set in their ways.

However, there is no such thing as a totally closed system. As long as it remains a vital entity (for as long as it exists), a second tendency pushes it toward growth and change. This growth feeds on the input, the new ideas, new knowledge, new people, new energy from both within and without the system and achieves its realization by using or processing this input, adapting it for its own use, and returning output. In a sense, the interaction between a system and its environment is the system's lifeline, without which it tends to spin its internal wheels, focus on maintaining its internal relationships unchanged, and become less and less effective as a working body. It is true that a healthy system is characterized by equilibrium, but it is a *dynamic* equilibrium between these two tendencies: the energy devoted to housekeeping, to keeping itself going, and the energy devoted to growing and working in its environment.

Each system exists within certain boundaries, across which flow the vital input and output. The interfaces between systems and subsystems, the points at which the boundaries touch, are areas crucial to effective functioning. The linkages that the system constructs across these interfaces will play a significant part in the subsystems' ability to work in unity. These interfaces are characterized by both competition and collaboration, which become obvious when looked at in light of the three major sources of conflict discussed earlier: conflict over different values, conflict over allocation of rewards and resources, and conflict over threats to existence. The tensions that exist at these interfaces can be either a healthy, growth-producing environment or destructive.

Competition and Collaboration

Competition between systems within an organization is destructive when the larger view is lost and the system is battling to maintain and promote itself, at any cost. This can be illustrated by events currently transpiring in university systems across the country due to financial pressures. Decisions are being made on which programs and which subsystems within the universities shall be retained, which expanded, and which abandoned. In this instance, valid decisions can only be made in light of dual perspectives: that of the value of the subsystem in and of itself as weighed against the worth of the other subsystems and as a contributing part of the whole, and that of the overall purpose of the university and the methods of achieving that purpose. This is especially true when available resources are limited, as they almost always are.

Competition, to be constructive, must be tempered by respect for the whole of which the system is a part. This demands not only a degree of personal selflessness on the part of the individuals involved but also a degree of system selflessness, based on enlightened and objective evaluation of the totality of the organization and its needs. Absence of this kind of enlightened objectivity can force the organization to make arbitrary decisions, without input from its various subsystems.

The other half of the action occurring along the interfaces of systems is collaboration. Organizations are constructed so that the various subsystems complement and supplement each other to create an effective whole and must work together in order to do so. There must be specific provision for communication and exchange between them. These planned linkages are illustrated in Figures 6 and 7, in which some individuals serve on two different teams to provide this kind of liaison. Provision for this is usually a part of the overall organizational plan, but failing this, the various subsystems should perceive the need and remedy the deficiency early in their cooperation.

Relationships Between Team and Host

In human service, the organization acts as a host to the team. It not only sanctions the work of the team but provides for its maintenance needs and usually affords it a "protective umbrella" in the community. The organization also determines overall purpose and policy, is responsible for executive decisions about how these policies shall apply to the team, and generally defines the nature and extent of team participation in organizational matters. The manner in which the organization carries out these tasks creates a climate that markedly affects the functioning of the team. Complex organizations tend to be explicitly structured: schedules and routines definite and carefully spelled out; goals, roles, and tasks specifically defined; territories delineated; and formal and hierarchical relationships the rule rather than the exception.

These characteristics are in contrast to the democratic team makeup, which appears to be the most productive type of team, but just as the organization affects the team, so the team can affect the organization. Because of the differences in size and power between team and organization, these effects may be hard to achieve, but organizational change is a major responsibility of the service team that is primarily involved with the client population, that is in a position to know and evaluate the needs and methods of providing service, and that has the expertise to determine what to do and how to do it. Actually, in many structured organizations, we find service teams that possess a so-called "inner freedom." Negotiations between team and organization should be ongoing, and their success appears to be contingent on the manner in which the following four concerns are dealt with.

1. There must be clear commitment to a common overall organization and team purpose, with acceptance of the fact that the contributions of each toward realizing this purpose, of necessity, differ. The organization's role is basically one of overall leadership and facilitation for the service team, which is charged with the provision of the service. While there is commonality of overall purpose, the goals and the means of reaching the goals may differ between organization and team.

Such disagreement can be illustrated by the current struggle in the public welfare program centering around use of computer technology as a tool in both service and in accountability. Modern public welfare has been divided into two programs: income maintenance, which involves providing funds for people whose sole need is money; and services, which provides actual assistance, such as housekeeping, health care, and consultation, for people who have problems other than financial. As a tool in planning and as a method of measurement of services and results, a classification form for services has been developed, in which workers in services categorize the problems with which they are working. There is considerable resistence on the part of workers to use of this as a tool, the basic criticisms being that it is not valid and that it represents an effort to put people into boxes without regard to the many human variables. This represents only one more aspect of the never to be totally resolved conflict between technology and humanity, and yet it can and will be negotiated, with hopefully a compromise agreed on.

2. There must be specific provision for channels of communication between the host organization and the team operating within its boundaries. The importance of this cannot be overstressed. There should be a constant flow of information back and forth in the form

of reports, worksheets, and memoranda, and there should be constant monitoring to determine that their content not only is being understood but is appropriate and timely. Frequently and tragically, the crucial moment for meaningful action is lost because of slowness and inadequacy of sharing information.

It is important, also, that there is personal contact between the team and the organization, not only on the part of the individual officially charged with liaison responsibility but on the part of other members. There is no substitute for people relating to people. The individual charged with the dual responsibility for being both a team member and an organization person usually has to deal with conflicting role demands. He will not only need to be capable of reconciling these but also capable of representing the specific concerns of both the team and the organization and of negotiating between the two. The rueful comment of the new Vice Chancellor of the University of Nebraska, concerning losing his departmental friends when assuming the new post, is a sad commentary on the inability of individuals in the system to understand and accept what is involved in this difficult dual role.

3. Provision must be made for autonomous exercise of judgment by team members whose expertise in their own area is such that this is both desirable and necessary. The basic premise on which teamwork rests is that there are differing bodies of knowledge and skill and that people cannot be competent in all areas. This autonomy does not mean that decisions are made without regard to the relationships among the team, the organization, and the overall organizational policy. Equally, the team should not be called upon to implement policies in the making of which it has no voice. For example, many physicians are deeply concerned with the fact that decisions on how long patients should be hospitalized are being made by hospital administrators and insurance companies, often without too much regard for the needs of the individual patient and the advice of the practicing physician. This is an area in which professional judgment does well to be weighed in light of other variables but still should be of primary importance.

Another area in which this negotiation between team and organization is of paramount importance lies in the selection of team members and the employment of personnel. It is the pattern in some organizations to employ a total team, as with the cancer research team that moves complete with physicians, geneticists, social workers, and technicians from one hospital to the other. The team, as well as the organization, needs to have a voice in who the members of the team are.

4. There must be adequate provision for accountability of the team to the host organization and for evaluation by the host organization of its effectiveness. In the final analysis, the organization is responsible for the team and its work. Clearly, there must be organizational understanding of what the team is doing and why, as well as measurement of its effectiveness.

Team Accountability

As discussed earlier, the whole question of accountability in human service is an extremely difficult one, particularly in the more intangible areas, where results are often only visible after many years and in terms of the total picture. We can demonstrate clearly, for instance, the success or lack of success of programs to wipe out polio, provide legal services for indigent people, teach children to read, and provide housekeeping service during a mother's illness. It is less easy to show the success or failure of, say, marriage counseling, where in the long run, the worker's help in keeping the marriage going could be destructive to both adults and children, or the success or failure of a program for delinquent adolescents that aspires not only to limit the delinquency but improve the client's feelings about himself. Human variables are infinite, and the instrument that measures the totality of man has not yet been devised.

Internal changes within people are not only difficult to achieve, they are difficult to demonstrate, and the assessment of their utility often can be only effectively carried out over a long period of time. Nevertheless, the work of the human service team must be responsibly conceived and executed, and evaluation is a part of this totality. It is first the task of the team itself and second of the host organization.

Of major concern at the present time, particularly in light of the current controversy over malpractice in medicine, is the question of legal accountability for team decisions. In medical teams, for example, this responsibility almost universally rests with the physician, but it is not nearly so clearly defined in teams in other areas. Who, for example, is legally responsible when the team working with a retarded child decides he is ready for a community living experience that results in his accidental injury or death? This area needs study.

The Team and the Community

The nature of the service team's involvement with the overall community in which it functions will, to a large extent, be determined by its purpose, by its position within the organization, and by the part it is designed to play in the overall picture. As pointed out earlier, one of the responsibilities of the host organization is to provide a "protective umbrella" for its teams, but the kinds of umbrella and the ways they are used vary widely.

In modern social planning, complex organizations are allotted a "catchment area," a specified region whose boundaries are determined by various factors: commonality of problem, geographic unity, similarity of social group, availability or lack of availability of service. One of the accepted ways of serving this catchment area is to establish satellite sections of the organization within specified districts of the region and assign a team total responsibility for provision of services there. This is a model widely used in public welfare programs on a state level, particularly in those states where large and isolated rural sections create problems in accessibility.

There are many advantages to the catchment type of social organization. In ensures involvement of local people, often the determining factor in success or failure; it allows for adaptation of program and services to unique local needs; it brings the service within reach of the client population; it allows for provision of a broad range of services designed to meet the needs of the total person; and it breaks down an area large and unmanageable in either size or population into a workable unit.

Community Teamwork

The catchment model is used in both rural and urban areas. The Y Street clinic is a good example of its use in an urban setting. On the basis of a soundly devised and implemented study, a certain area was designated as a high-risk maternal and child health district. This was a part of the city where most of the employment had been in packing houses, and when they were automated, although an effort was made to retrain and find new jobs for the employees, the rate of family breakdown, particularly in the more marginal units, was high. As a part of total community planning, the city's Comprehensive Health Center designated a basic outreach team, consisting of a physician, social worker, and community organizer, to go into this area and develop a facility to meet the needs of the people there.

The potential for success of this team rested on its ability to understand and relate to the needs, wishes, and expectations of the people in the neighborhood. Initial steps, therefore, involved a series of discussions and meetings with a broad range of local people, designed to determine their needs and develop some sort of formal or informal neighborhood association to participate in the work of the team and act as a primary liaison between the people and the service personnel. In these meetings, there was general exploration of patterns of neighborhood functioning, of the power and communication structures, of the existence and importance of various subgroups and social resources such as churches and schools, as well as consideration of specifics in types of services needed and wanted, location of facility, transportation, hours, specialized personnel, funding. There was, as well, a beginning effort to pinpoint tensions and sore points within the neighborhood.

On this groundwork, the facility itself was established and its program developed with constant back-and-forth communication between it and the neighborhood as well as the total city. Of equal importance was the team's involvement with its host organization, which provided the major part of the funding and set overall policy and purpose, from which the team's own purpose was derived. Other subsystems were developed, from which were drawn consulting specialists whom the team called for such services as family planning, specialized medicine and psychiatry, provision of educational resources, and so on. As need became obvious, this initial team expanded to include other specialists. Of particular importance to its success were the aides, the indigenous workers whose life experiences were the key element in their preparation for the job and whose formal training was on an inservice level. They constituted the first line of communication with many of the neighborhood people and were vital to the work of the team.

The Y Street team carried responsibility for its own relationship with the community outside the host organization. It planned and sold its own program to the general public and to the consumers of the service. Another team within the same host organization had virtually no primary responsibility for its relationship with the overall community except through the people it served. This was the Abortion Counseling team within the OB-GYN service of the Comprehensive Health Center (general hospital). This team, consisting of physician, nurse, and social worker, operated within the hospital itself, relating to the other service subsystems there and to the hospital administration, its host organization. This was a sensitive issue, both in the community and in the overall governing board of the hospital; thus the interpretation of the program and the allocation of resources not only required considerable ongoing time and involvement but had implications for the operation of the total center. Therefore, the host organization carried primary responsibility, with representation from the team as necessary.

Relationships Among Team, Organization, and Community

In the eyes of the public, the service team always represents the host organization and vice versa. President Truman's classic comment on the buck stopping at his desk is applicable to the overall organization being held responsible by the community for service teams operating under its aegis. The community sanctions both, through use of services and through support, and although it delegates to the organization responsibility for policy-making regarding purpose and method of achieving purpose, this is expressive of a framework of accepted values and norms on which continued sanction is contingent. The organization *is* accountable to the community for actions of its subsystems. Not infrequently, the method of providing service that is developed and used by the team runs counter to accepted community standards and norms, and the organization finds itself in the middle of a controversy between the two. It is important that the channels between the team and the host organization are open and that there is common understanding and agreement on what is being done, why, and how. Differences of opinion between the two should be worked out as part of "housekeeping" before facing the community. The degree of autonomy granted the team for developing and interpreting its own program and raising its own funds should be related to the degree of openness and communication between host and team.

The triad—community, organization, service team—has a certain built-in potential for conflict in light of two factors that are increasingly significant in our restless society: (1) the emphasis on fundamental social change and social justice and (2) the proliferation of knowledge on the nature of man.

Impetus for development of the great human service systems—medicine, law, education, nursing, social work—derives from the society itself. Recognizing that problems and unmet needs exist, the society develops organizations for dealing with them, but these organizations are conceived within the framework of the society's values and norms and, as such, are constituted to maintain the status quo. The organizations, in turn, develop bodies of knowledge on which the expertise of their practitioners rests, and that knowledge increasingly is saying that man's problems cannot be dealt with nor his needs met without basic change in the very society that is the progenitor of the human service systems.

Increasingly, human service organizations see their role as prevention and maximization of potential rather than remediation, recognizing that under present circumstances, human problems develop faster and more comprehensively than they can be treated and that they cannot be dealt with effectively in an unchanged society. Awareness and acceptance of this and committment to the role of change agent has given human service organizations the dilemma of maintaining the support and sanction of a system whose basic nature they are attempting to change.

Equally controversial are some of the practice methods developed by service personnel. In sanctioning the organization, the community delegates responsibility for selection of methods, in a sense saying that the professionals are people who know more and better how to realize the purpose than the general public. However, the society retains the right to question methods and withdraw its sanction—and frequently does. The public school system is particularly vulnerable to this kind of attack, periodically evident in controversies over bussing, selection of textbooks, and in some areas, use of behavior modification techniques to assist parents and teachers in altering harmful student behavior patterns. The result is that programs are often discontinued before they are really tested to determine success or failure.

The team must carry within it not only the goals and desires of its host organization but also those of the society to which it is ultimately responsible. At the team's interfaces with these two systems, it should plan that specific linkages be open for objective analysis and evaluation of feedback so that it can deal with incipient problems before they mushroom in size. Or on a conscious, planned basis, the team should use the tension and openness to change created by a crisis to facilitate change both within the team and within the society. Without this, the team is vulnerable to abrupt withdrawal of sanction and termination of its efforts. The arena of human service is littered with corpses of well-intentioned projects, aborted due to lack of understanding of what was being attempted—a futile, wasteful process. The society has not only the responsibility but the right to question what is being done; the team that forgets this does so at its own peril.

Related Readings

Anderson, Ralph and Carter, Irl: Human Behavior in the Social Environment. Chicago: Aldine Publishing Co., 1974.
   Useful and readable text that attempts to correlate human development with factors in the social system, using material from different disciplines.
Cox, Fred, *et al.*: Strategies of Community Organization. Itasca, Ill.: Peacock Publishers, 1970.
   Good collection of basic well-written articles on working with organizations, neighborhoods, and communities.
Etzione, Amitai: Modern Organizations. Englewood Cliffs, N.J.: Prentice-Hall, 1964.
   Good basic text in development and current status of social organizations.
Hearn, Gordon (Editor): The General Systems Approach—Contributions Toward a Holistic Conception of Social Work. New York: Council on Social Work Education, 1968.
   Well-written understandable, and practical essays on adapting concepts from systems theory to the demands of practice.
Katz, David and Kahn, Robert: The Social Psychology of Organizations. New York: John Wiley, 1966.
   A review of the basic dynamics of organizations.

Kraslow, Florence, *et al.*: Issues in Human Services. San Francisco: Jossey-Bass, 1972.

Emphasis on changing administrative practices and staffing patterns as they affect practice in social organizations.

Lippit, Ronald; Watson, Jeanne and Westley, Bruce: The Dynamics of Planned Change. New York: Harcourt Brace, 1958.

Basic and useful reading regarding the underlying processes involved in social change.

Weissman, Harold: Overcoming Mismanagement in the Human Service Profes- sions. San Francisco: Jossey-Bass, 1973.

One individual's struggle with changing a social system

CHAPTER 8

ThE WORkiNG TEAM

Modern teamwork is essentially a task-oriented approach to problem-solving. It rests on a logical progression, as illustrated by Figure 8, which begins with a definition of the problem and the purpose and proceeds to detail the goals, tasks, roles, and interventions, then evaluates and revises, if necessary. To help display this progression, a problem will be defined and followed through the various problem-solving steps in this chapter.

The Problem-Solving Process

Problem

Human service systems are designed with a threefold objective: to maximize human potential, to prevent breakdown in people's social functioning, and to remedy human suffering. The extent and range of possible problems encompassed by these overall aims are vast. Furthermore, problems rare-

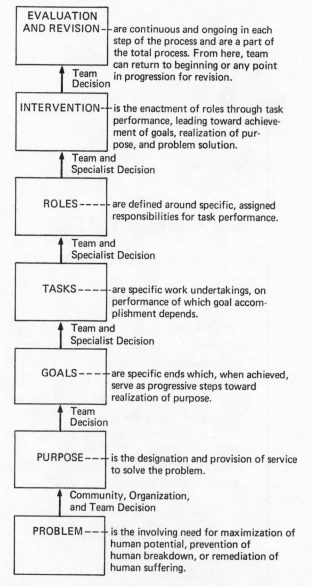

Figure 8. Steps in the Problem-Solving Process of Human Service Teams

ly occur separately and are usually related and contribute to one another's origin and expansion, so that we are generally faced with a cluster of interrelated problems, any one of which has aspects of each category.

Adequate human nutrition, for example, according to recent

research findings, holds the key to many normal developmental phases and also thereby determines the capacity of people for social functioning and, when absent, can cause considerable suffering. The problem thus exists at once on all three levels.

While the presence of various specialists on a team makes it possible to encompass a much broader range of services and include those that are at once facilitative, preventive, and remedial, defining the problem in a way that is too global, too ambitious, and nonspecific can lead to a diffusion of effort, which is not productive of the desired result.

In the late nineteenth and early twentieth centuries, the heyday of important breakthroughs in understanding the human condition, all things seemed possible, including complete cure for human problems. The sobering realization that this promise could not be fulfilled, that the very nature of man makes it impossible, introduced a trend toward a more realistic appraisal of the dimensions of the problem-to-be-solved, in the light of possible solutions. Modern research has pointed out that, while comprehension of problem dimension is essential, limitation of focus based on what realistically is achievable with available resources is equally essential.

The initial step in the process of teamwork, then, is defining the problem to be dealt with, its dimensions and its boundaries. In a sense, this is a process of cutting the problem down to a workable size. For maximum results, this undertaking is jointly shared by the host organization and the team itself and frequently by the community. The extent and nature of the problem will determine whether the team model should be used, so this is the initial decision, most frequently made by the organization, often on the recommendation of individual practitioners, and frequently with input from the community. The organization also first defines the problem, in terms of its own policy and program and its position in the network of community services. This definition should be subject to modification by the team of specialists, from whose input may come limitation, expansion, or change of focus. This process of evaluation of problem definition should result in all team members being very clear and specific about the nature of the need they are trying to meet.

For many years, solution of the problems posed by mental retardation consisted of institutionalization, but in the past quarter century, largely as an outgrowth of the efforts of parents, the emphasis has changed to one of normalization, wherein retardates are retained in or returned to the community, and special programs to meet their differential needs are developed. *The problem then, can be defined as inadequate and noneffective services for retardates in light of new knowledge and skill.* Retardation, in and of itself, is a multifaceted problem, requiring the services of many different experts, and such a comprehensive change of view lends itself naturally to a team approach.

Purpose

Out of the definition of the problem comes a statement of the purpose of the team, *i.e.*, the specific design and method of provision of service leading to problem solution. The purpose determines the structure of the team (how it is organized); its composition (who is included); its size (how many members); and its working method (the operating procedures). It is thus mandatory that the purpose be clearly and commonly understood and accepted by both the team members and the overall institution, as it constitutes the focal point for all work. Without this clarity of understanding, efforts can lose direction and become mutually contradictory and ineffectual. The purpose is a calculated statement of the results the team intends to achieve.

Out of our problem of inadequate and noneffective services for retardates, in light of new knowledge and skills arises a very clear purpose—*to develop and operationalize normalization programs and services that would enable the retardate to achieve maximum independence in living.*

Goals

The goals arise out of the purpose and become the intermediate and complementary steps taken on the way to achievement of the purpose. As such, they constitute a progression; one goal, when achieved, leads to the next. Understandably, then, a major team undertaking is visualizing the goals and setting priorities among them. The goals should be specific and realizable and, for maximum results, should exist on a timetable.

In setting priorities in human service, it is essential to keep in mind the theory of emergent needs, which states that basic human needs must be met first. It is a sad reality that it usually takes a crisis of some sort to force individuals and societies to take steps to remedy a bad situation that usually has been festering for a long time.

For example, three consecutive suicides within a short period of time in "the hole" in a penitentiary finally kicked off an effort to provide better facilities.

The initial goal must always be dealing with the immediate crisis, be it child abuse, illness, starvation. Only when the present reality is under control can we expect people to become involved in working on the extended goals, even though the realization of long-term goals might have greater effect in the long run than dealing with the immediate crisis. This concept is basic in education for human service, but it is a source of considerable conflict for workers, who frequently find themselves in the frustrating position of dealing only with immediate and demanding emergencies. It is a source of comfort to know that these periods of crisis present opportunity for capitalization on work that offers maximum effectiveness; people and societies are more open to change when they are off balance in a crisis.

> From our purpose (to develop and operationalize normalization programs and services that will enable the retardate to achieve maximum independence in living) arise a variety of goals: *(1) building adequate community understanding and support; (2) securing funds; (3) designing adequate programs and facilities; (4) differential evaluation of the retarded persons; and (5) direct work with individuals and families.*

Realization of each goal depends on the performance of certain tasks which are implicit in the goal and become explicit through its formulation. The goal is only realizable through these various specific job undertakings.

Tasks

The team's development and critical examination of the goals arising from its purpose will involve recognition of and provision for the necessary correlation of tasks but will also define their specific boundaries.

> Our goals of building community support, securing funding, developing programs, evaluating consumers, and working directly with consumers spell out the following tasks: *(1) planning and opening channels of meaningful communication within the community, using various media; (2) exploring possible sources of funds, preparing sample budgets, writing*

*grant requests, and correlating funding with those of other local programs;
(3) surveying other such programs and facilities as well as local conditions
and resources and correlating both aspects of such surveys; (4) testing for
and assembling factual data regarding the retarded person and his unique
situation in light of both his needs and available resources; (5) working
with the individual client and his family to construct the bridges necessary
to enable them to use the changing programs.*

Roles

When the tasks implicit in the goals have been visualized and designated, when the team is clear as to *what* needs to be done, the *who*
should become obvious. The nature of teaming is such that, while
roles are designated and assigned on the basis of specialization, the
factor of personal "fitness" for the demands of the role can be
taken into consideration, and varying combinations of tasks can be
included in a particular role. The educator mentioned in the list of
roles below, for example, might possess particular equipment and
skills for lobbying and could be used in that role, also. Such flexibility of assignment affords the team the ability to utilize its personnel for maximum effectiveness.

The specialized roles indicated by the tasks spelled out in the retardation
problem would include: *(1) a community organizer; (2) an educator;
(3) a physician; (4) a psychologist; (5) a social worker; (6) a speech therapist; (7) a physiotherapist; (8) a lobbyist; (9) parents; (10) house parents;
(11) volunteers.*

Some of these roles would obviously overlap, and negotiation
would be necessary. Equally obvious, in so complex an organization,
there would be a point at which the original planning team would
give birth to a number of smaller teams, each with its own designated
problem and purpose and existing as a subsystem within the total,
larger system.

Evaluation and Revision

The progression of problem-solving via the team model in human service utilizes the classic scientific method of study: recognition and
systematic formulation of a problem; collection of data surrounding
the problem through observation and experimentation; development
and testing of tentative hypotheses or explanations of the problem;

and the emergence of a valid theory or law on which practice principles can be built.

When the tasks have been assigned and the roles designated, the team member proceeds to act on the basis of both team decisions and his individual specialized judgment. His actions, as well as the actions of the team, and the results of both are subject to continuous scrutiny and ongoing evaluation and revision. Without this, the whole process loses its vitality and validity. This means that there must be provision not only for dissemination of information about what is going on but also built-in requirements and opportunities for feedback/feedforward and commitment to responsible, critical examination of the work being done.

Meetings and Discussion

Work progression and problem-solving through the team model rest on mastery of two basic skills: use of meetings and use of their essential corollary, discussion. These are the tools the team uses in reaching the vital decisions of who will do what, why, when, where, how and in fitting the answers into a meaningful pattern, assessing and evaluating that pattern, and when necessary, changing it. Misuse of these two fundamental skills is at the root of many of the classic complaints about the team model—that it is time-consuming, unwieldy, and unable to act. These problems are not inherent in the team model but arise from a lack of the knowledge and ability to use meetings and discussion wisely and with maximum effectiveness.

Meetings

Good team meetings can be formal or informal, scheduled or non-scheduled. They can take place, with equal effectiveness, in the steaming, noisy laundry room of a hospital or in the quiet sanctum of a twentieth-story, walnut-panelled boardroom. Team meetings represent, in a sense, the classic "peak of the iceberg," in that they constitute the apex, the bringing together of many different elements. It is possible to identify five of these elements as having major significance: (1) disciplined and mature participation of team members; (2) adequate dissemination of information; (3) advance preparation; (4) organization within the meeting; (5) parsimonious use of time.

The team member prepares himself for participation in the

meeting both by performance of his unique role of specialist operating individually and in his role as part of the team process. Initially,
he must be committed to use of the meeting. With the tremendous
time demands on very specialized practitioners, such as physicians,
and with lack of sophistication and skill in effective use of meetings,
this commitment is sometimes difficult to achieve. Experiential
learning in meeting use and demonstration of its potential for time-
saving and greater effectiveness can overcome this attitude and
generate enthusiasm and ability to work in meetings. Knowledgeable
leadership in use of meetings can also be of great help here.

Meaningful participation of team members rests not only on
committment but also on advance preparation, be it collection and
assessment of data and preparing specialized recommendations for
team action; intervening in the client system and being prepared to
report on and evaluate the results of intervention; or familiarizing
oneself with information about other individual and team actions.
Because busy practitioners often do not find time to read and react
to written data in preparation for the meeting, some teams find it
necessary to make a rule that no member can participate in the discussion who has not read the material beforehand. This eliminates
unnecessary repetition of a time-consuming nature and subsequent
loss of attention.

The team whose members consistently come late and unprepared
to meetings has some unfinished business to deal with in its struggle
to reach maturity and will need to devote some time and energy to
working toward a solution of these problems. Nothing is more
destructive to morale or contributes more to breakdown in teaming
than the lack of responsible advance preparation or the frequent
absences of members.

A second aspect of advance preparation has to do with the supporting structure in which the team works. This involves provision of
time, place, concrete resources, secretarial services, if necessary, and,
in current times, refreshments, usually coffee. This latter serves the
same purpose as small talk at the beginning of an interview; it allows
for a brief and relaxed coming together prior to moving into a pattern
of work. Like the interview, refreshments can be useful and effective
if not prolonged or too elaborate.

Good meetings require adequate dissemination of information, a
major problem in complex organizations in spite of our highly
sophisticated technology for reproduction and circulation of data.
Not only must the information be prepared and communicated in a

form that is meaningful to the users, it must be circulated in advance, allowing sufficient time for consumption and digestion by the users. All too frequently, participants are greeted at a meeting with hand-outs, which for adequate use, should have been circulated days prior to the meeting. An additional factor in information preparation, retrieval, and use is the sheer volume of such material that inundates the team member in human service daily. This is an area in which the promised increased efficiency of a more sophisticated technology has not yet materialized, and team members can only struggle with a variety of systems that do not always work, alone or together. This is one of the major problems confronting effective use of team meetings, and the team should devote time to developing a system that best meets its own needs.

Even if participants are committed and disciplined and fully prepared to utilize the meeting to best advantage, without organization within the meeting itself to ensure structure and movement, the result can be aimless and ineffectual. A written agenda can be useful in setting the stage, and ready access to resources (writing materials, audiovisual devices, etc.) will facilitate matters. The type of leadership available will also effect the success of the meeting. In the early life of the team, the leader may need to assume greater responsibility for organizing, clarifying, and summarizing—being responsible for the team members' learning to use the meeting, but as the team matures and its skill in meeting develops, the need for imposed structure lessens.

Finally, the factors of time and timing are important in successful use of meetings. As a rule of thumb, we can say that no meeting should be held without a specific purpose and a specific time allocation for the anticipated achievement of that purpose. The focus that derives from a clearly stated and understood purpose will contribute to movement, to limitation of discussion to that which is pertinent, and to prompt decision-making. There should be time for maximum participation, but only as related to the subject at hand. A meeting should never be held just because it has been scheduled, and periodically, need for and use of team meetings should be reevaluated.

Discussion

The major medium of communication in a meeting is discussion, and the pattern it follows promotes or detracts from the team's ability to utilize its greatest capacity for achievement. This pattern may vary according to the purpose of the meeting, but in general, the form that encourages greatest interpersonal communication is best. Discussion patterns are influenced greatly by the physical arrangement of the group, the familiar circle, which enables participants to see and relate to all, generally being the most desirable.

We can designate four patterns of discussion, as illustrated in Figure 9: recitation, discussion, confidential conversations, subgroup discussions, and open discussion.

Recitation discussion is used when teaching or imparting of information is the major purpose. The channels of communication run between teacher or leader and student or participant with a minimum of interaction from the other members of the group. While useful in specific instances, in team meetings that stress the importance of participation, it tends to be counterproductive, resulting in low group morale, a low level of participation, and little feeling of personal or team responsibility. The setup for this type of discussion usually places the teacher/leader apart from the remainder of participants on a podium, which is conducive to little interaction.

Interpersonal confidential conversations, which take place between members within the group, are not at all uncommon but do not contribute to the development and effectiveness of the team. They usually involve content that the participants, for many reasons, do not want to share with other team members, content inappropriate to the purpose of the meeting. Confidential conversations may signal the effort of the particular members involved to disassociate themselves from what is taking place. Such conversations thus tend to be disruptive and cause breakdown in overall communication.

Multilevel subgroup discussions grow out of the tendency of members to establish communication with people who share their positions with regard to status and power and their interests and points of view. When this occurs, most of the significant conversation and decision-making are controlled by the highest status/power group, and the team does not function on democratic principles, as desired.

Open discussion is characterized by input from all, by use of feedback, and by maximum interpersonal communication. It grows out of a climate of openness and respect for the contributions of all team members and represents maximum team functioning.

These four patterns do not represent absolutes in the sense that they are mutually exclusive. Most team discussions will include some

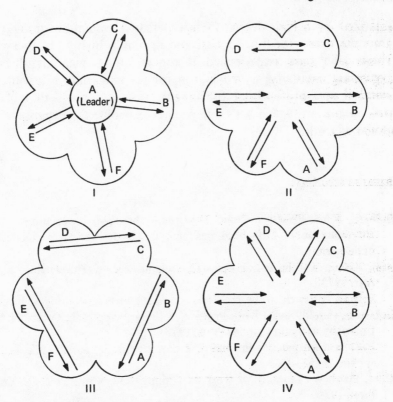

Figure 9. Discussion Patterns on a Six-Member Team
I, Recitation Discussion: The leader controls participation by recognizing speakers, restating and reshaping comments, asking questions, summarizing, and concluding. Little or no team interaction is involved.
II, Interpersonal Confidential Conversations: Two or more individuals talk with each other, excluding the leader and/or other team members; there is limited team interaction. In this diagram, D and C are involved in such a discussion.
III, Multi-Level Subgroup Discussion: A and B, the high-level members; C and D, the middle-level members; and E and F, the low-level members, talk significantly only to each other. Fragmented discussion and limited interaction occur.
IV, Open Discussion: There is shared input from all members and maximum interaction.

elements of each, as appropriate to the matter under consideration. This can be done without danger to the essential pattern of democratic discussion, but the team that falls into using patterns other than open discussion to any large degree would do well to look at its own functioning.

A good meeting with good discussion—a meeting of minds characterized by a high degree of interpersonal communication—represents the team model at its best and results in highly creative work. Those who have experienced it report on its meaningfulness in expanding creativity, as a medium for learning, and as a source of personal and professional fulfillment. It is a process that can be learned and, in fact, *must* be if we are to realize the promise of this model of work.

Related Readings

Brilhard, John: Effective Group Discussion. Dubuque, Iowa: Brown, 1967.
  Extremely useful little book dealing with the down-to-earth practicalities of discussion.
Brill, Naomi: Working with People—The Helping Process. Philadelphia: Lippincott, 1973.
  Eclectic approach to the problems and possibilities in working with people.
Goldstein, Harold: Social Work Practice, A Unitary Approach. Columbia, S.C.: University of South Carolina Press, 1973.
  Basic text on practice in human service, specifically social work, within a systems framework.
Miles, Matthew: Learning to Work in Groups. New York: Teachers' College Press, 1959.
  Extremely useful basic text on working with other members within a team structure.
Osborn, Parker *et al.*: Consultation, A Review of the Literature. Denver: University of Denver School of Social Work, 1971, unpublished.
  Survey and analysis of the literature on consultation in eight different disciplines, good bibliography.
Overton, Alice, *et al.*: Casework Notebook of the St. Paul Family Centered Project. St. Paul, Minn.: Greater St. Paul Community Chests and Councils, 1959.
  Old but excellent report on pioneer effort to deal with totality of situation.
Pincus, Allen and Minihan, Anne: Social Work Practice, Model and Method. Itasca, Ill.: Peacock Publishers, 1973.
  Well-written and usable text on application of concepts from systems theory in social work practice; broadly applicable to human services and to teamwork.
Reid, William and Epstein, Laura: Task-Centered Casework. New York: Columbia University Press, 1972.
  Focus on practice models geared to task performance.

Thielen, Herbert A.: Dynamics of Groups at Work. Chicago: University of Chicago Press, 1963.

Excellent analysis of process in working groups.

Weissman, Harold, *et al.*: Individual and Group Services in the Mobilization for Youth Experiences. New York: Association Press, 1969.

Practical application of small group theory in helping young people maximize potential.

Wise, Harold *et al.*: Making Health Teams Work. Cambridge, Mass.: Ballinger Publishing Co., 1974.

A must—practical and well-written paperback on the day-to-day struggle involved in making the team model work.

CHAPTER 9

EducATioN foR TEAMWORK

The problems of team practice are serious. The central one is the behavior of the team members. Social workers and the professionals in other disciplines within the school do not know how to work well together.*

This rueful comment is echoed over and over in the literature and in talking with people who are seriously attempting to use the team model in service delivery. All too frequently, teamwork degenerates into a form of parallel play, such as seen in two-year-olds, the team members working contiguous to each other but not actually *with* each other and the resulting effort never jelling into a balanced whole created by the total team as a result of the members' interactions with each other. The potential of the team model for synthesis and integration of knowledge and skill to produce more effective service, to provide both stimulation and learning for the various members, and to foster creativity goes unrealized. The role demands are complex and extensive, and it is

*Richard Anderson, "School Social Work: The Promise of a Team Model," *Child Welfare*, Vol. 53, no. 8 (October 1974): 528.

obvious that special learning in areas of both team membership and leadership are needed to enable workers and organizations to use the team effectively. Only with adequately trained personnel can the model itself be adequately tested.

Preparing Team Members

In examining the factors that contribute to the effective use of team-work, we can perceive three groups of workers involved at present. These groupings are applicable on all levels of education and training. They include: (1) those whose experience antedates current use of teams and whose major identification is with a hierarchical plan of organization and work; (2) those who are primarily oriented and committed to working on a personal, one-to-one basis; (3) those who are only beginning their careers and require education for participation in group endeavors. In all three of these groupings, the need for specialized and additional learning is obvious.

Education

The most important objective in any educational program for practitioners is the production of flexible workers, possessed of a learner's orientation and yet sufficient knowledge to actualize that orientation. Because of the complex and changing demands of team practice, because of the necessity for constant self-evaluation and self-renewal, personal and professional flexibility assume even greater importance. In teamwork, conscious use of the self in relationships with others is mandatory. As always, the worker's effectiveness rests on his ability to use his knowledge, which, regardless of how comprehensive, is of little meaning if he cannot participate in a joint operation with others.

In addition to this personal qualification, however, there is a growing body of "hard" knowledge about working in teams, without which the worker is often not even aware of the complexity of the model he is attempting to use. As one worker questioned, "How do you actually know what is going on in a group?" The knowledge we are developing attempts to answer this query and thus poses the team member with a responsibility for securing an ongoing education in it.

There are strong and encouraging movements in primary and

secondary school systems and in the informal learning settings involved in childhood education, such as the churches and recreation programs, in which democratic groupwork is stressed. In time, these efforts should result in a group of young people who are better prepared for meeting the demanding relationship roles of teamwork. At present, the required learning is primarily on an adult level.

The undergraduate and graduate programs that prepare students for human service are only beginning to recognize and consciously stress teamwork as a part of their educational offerings. Much of the learning, whether informal and deriving from attitudes of faculty members and class structure or formal in terms of teaching content, prepares the student to be unfit rather than fit for teamwork. All too often, a part of the acculturation process in professional schools is indoctrination in the belief that the discipline being taught is the most important and therefore the dominant one; that its specialized knowledge equips the possessor to be an expert in other areas about which he frequently has only a smattering of learning; that his participation in interdisciplinary work should automatically involve him in the leadership role.

Such attitudes are seen with disturbing frequency among faculty members and in the various departments on college campuses, where only lip service has been given to interdisciplinary education for nearly half a century. Departments are often willing to participate in such programs only when they are under the aegis of the department itself or when forced to do so by financial necessity or administrative dictum. In the latter instance, the resulting "shotgun marriages" can be uneasy, to put it mildly. This means that in order to effectively educate students for teamwork and, in order to provide the models and demonstrate the behaviors, faculties will first have to educate themselves.

Social/Organizational Climate

All too often, the attitudes mentioned above are reinforced by a society that endows certain practitioners with omniscience. Physicians, ministers, and, in some instances, lawyers are highly subject to this kind of social pressure when clients turn to them for guidance and help in areas in which they are not competent. The results can be tragic, as in those classic instances of parents, concerned by early evidence of disturbed behavior in a child, being advised that "he will grow out of it," without recognition by the advisor that there is a whole body of expert knowledge in these areas, on the basis of which it can be determined whether such reassurance is valid.

Learning for teamwork requires not only willingness to recognize the need for and the actual limitations on individual expertise but also the willingness and ability to recognize and respect expertise in others and to share clients with others. The team experience itself is pregnant with possibilities for this kind of learning, much of which can take place on the job.

The organization which opts to use the team model will need to develop concurrent educational programs as well as create and maintain a climate that is conducive to maximum involvement in them.

The importance of the "learning climate" is pointed out by findings of various studies on the effect of patterns of social structure on human experience. The phenomenon dubbed "situational adjustment" (individuals take on characteristics required by the situations in which they participate) affords a beginning point for such education. These studies postulate that out of such situational adjustment comes socialization in and commitment to new patterns of attitude and behavior.

When the organization and team climate are such that maximum learning and openness to change are an accepted part of the mores and when there is recognition and reward for such effort, workers tend to fall in with these patterns and become committed to them. Such a climate is encouraged by a variety of factors. Organizational management based on the theory that people can and do enjoy working, that they want to perform effectively, and that they tend to seek responsibility and a share in planning and decision-making seems to be most conducive to good morale and to development of the attitudes that encourage the risk-taking involved in learning and change. People tend to resist that which is forced on them, and it is a long way from mandatory compliance to acceptance and maximum utilization; people tend to react positively to that in which they have a participatory function; when there is understanding on why ongoing learning is necessary and a need felt for the changes it invokes, workers will find it easier to go along with its additional demands on them—recognition of these principles will enable the organization to design a program that has a chance of success.

Individual Characteristics

A National Institute of Mental Health summary of research relating to the individual characteristics that affect response to innovation and willingness and ability to learn new ways of thinking and working points out six important variables: age, economic status, personal sense of security, successfulness, cosmopolitanism, and professionalism. In considering these, it is well to remember that each worker represents a unique combination of them and that no one variable can be considered except in light of the others.

It is interesting to note, for instance, that while most research tends to indicate that younger people are more open to innovation than older people, there is at least one study which indicates that younger and older people are more open to change than those in the middle age range, who tend to be more "tradition-minded." Perhaps this is indicative of our growing understanding of what aging is and our changing social attitudes toward older people.

The economic status of the worker is a potent factor in determining not only personal rigidity but also motivation to hang on to what one has because of a desperate need for it. When change involves risking the concrete elements on which life itself depends, it is asking a great deal of an individual to demand that he learn new ways that perhaps he cannot master or that he participate in developing new programs in which there is perhaps no place for him. It would be an oversight to dismiss this factor without some consideration of the problems that exist due to inequities in rewards for work within organizations. Justifications for these inequities are based on competence, assignments and responsibilities, and educational demands, but these are valid as reasons for *differences* in rewards only. The major problem, which reflects our overall social problem, is that rewards on the lower end of the continuum are too small and on the higher end, too great.

The creation of democratically operating teams in an organization that includes, for example, employees who must moonlight because compensation for their work is too small and workers whose salaries quadruple those of others is difficult, to put it mildly. Such an unbalanced situation contributes to excessive application of the previously mentioned "Peter Principle," which states that workers vie for greater rewards and promotion up the ladder to the point where they function ineffectually, and there they remain. In human service systems, this problem is demonstrated by those excellent clinicians who become poor administrators in order to secure better salaries and more status.

In any ranking of basic human needs in order of their importance in affecting human behavior, the subsistence needs are first. Meeting them adequately and fairly is fundamental to creation of a personal sense of security, without which the worker will have trouble exercising the necessary flexibility to participate in and use changes. The worker who fears loss of employment, loss of status or prestige, or exposure of his own inadequacies may find the questioning of old ways and the developing of new ways threatening.

The factor of successfulness as a variable in affecting readiness for change is two-edged. The worker who is doing well and is satisfied with his employment may fear to lose by a change, but this will be somewhat balanced by his confidence in his own ability to take advantage of new experiences. This attitude is apparently reinforced if the worker has had the advantage of a variety of experiences, both personal and working, in which he has learned to be comfortable with and make use of different ways of thinking, working, and living—the factor of cosmopolitanism.

The final variable, professionalism, involves that commitment to ongoing learning that is a part of professional education. Resting on the truism that knowledge is constantly developing (being added to and changing in light of new understandings and situations), at its best, professionalism strives to develop openness, readiness, and strong motivation to seek ongoing education. The development of a questing mind and spirit, along with mastery of the tools that make its use possible, is the major achievement of a preparatory program for work in human service.

In addition to keeping these variables in mind, the organization developing and promoting an education program can utilize the concept of balance that is a fundamental attribute of both individuals and social systems. In both, there exists an ambivalence, a need both to change and to retain the status quo, and this can be recognized and capitalized on in developing motivation to participate meaningfully. Concrete rewards, such as promotions and extra pay, as incentives for effort can be useful, but most important is the creation of that climate oriented to change that reinforces the need for change and tips the balance in that direction. Crisis in an organization, a breakdown in functioning, creating tension, imbalance, and questioning of the status quo can be extremely useful, but by and large, an ongoing, educational program as an accepted part of day-to-day operation, as well as the experiential, on-the-job learning that derives from participation in the process itself are essential elements in enabling present-day human service workers to test out and use the various team models of practice that are developing.

Knowledge of Self, Group and Specialty

Given existence of the desired climate and the readiness to develop and use ongoing educational programs, the question naturally arises as to the kinds of experiences that are most effective in preparing people for teamwork. Three different levels of knowledge are necessary for teamworkers: basic knowledge of self in relationship with others, generalized knowledge relating to social and group dynamics, and specialized knowledge in a particular area.

Basic knowledge of self in relationship with others and the ability to use this knowledge constructively is unique and individual. Teams vary greatly, both in the extent to which development of this kind of knowledge is a formal goal of team operation and in the manner in which they endeavor to promote it. While ideally a flexible, non-defensive self is most useful in teamwork, individuals differ markedly in their capacity for this kind of functioning. The strong team has ability to adapt to these kinds of differences, unless they are extreme. The specialist whose expertise is indispensible may be a "rigid digit," with a low toleration for other people and little ability to know himself. Knowing this, the team can compensate in various ways, learn to deal with the situation as constructively as possible, and develop the balanced whole that is the effective team. In their efforts, they can be buoyed up by both the knowledge that the longer people work together, the more they find that they can get along with each other, as well as the conviction that people possess the capacity for change and growth—even rigid digits!

There are extremes in personality, however, that make individuals unfit for teamwork, and when there is well-demonstrated inability to change these, it may be necessary to remove that person from the team and use his expertise in some other way. The individual whose personality needs are so great and uncontrolled that he is destroying the team itself by divisiveness, manipulation, dishonesty, must be dealt with. Ideally, he should not be in human service. Actually, he exists and accordingly must be realistically dealt with.

This kind of knowledge derives more from experiential than academic sources and should be spread across the whole spectrum of education. There is no substitute for actually experiencing the range of behaviors that take place in group interaction. Without conscious effort to understand and use these experiences, however, they may be nothing more than a source of frustration. They should be supplemented by work on both individual and group levels, so that workers can move from intuitive behavior that in some instances may be quite effective but without understanding or control to a conscious use of behavior to achieve predictable effects.

The generalized knowledge relating to social and group dynamics consists of theories and derived techniques relating to:

1. The nature of society, not only in terms of the way it develops and its present trends, but also as reflected concretely in the specific social units in which the team operates: urban, rural, city, state, county.

2. The nature (structure, dynamics, and operation) of both simple and complex organizations.

3. Social psychology and small group dynamics, encompassing what is known about the forces that operate among people in groups.

4. Open communication, with special emphasis on the factors that contribute to and impede its effectiveness.

5. Problem-solving, both within and without the team, as an orderly, disciplined process.

While general awareness and understanding of these various bodies of knowledge is essential for all team members, the amount and degree needed will vary according to the role of the individual on the team. The team will be stronger, for example, if all individuals possess knowledge of what is involved in leadership, but the person responsible for its exercise will need to be master of its use to a greater extent. A democracy requires a high degree of "literacy" among its members, and a democratic team is no exception to this rule. Without some understanding of what is involved, the team member will truly not "know what is going on" and will be subject to manipulation and be unable to participate effectively.

Finally, specialized knowledge, that concentrated, differential know-how that qualifies the expert to fill his unique place on the team, is the third essential type of knowledge. Because of great demand for the services of highly trained specialists, the trend is to assess skills in terms of what *only* the specialist can do and conserve his or her time for these tasks. One advantage of the team model is that the overlap of knowledge and skill becomes obvious, and assignments can be made in such a way as to use expertise in the most economic fashion. As the specialist, who is usually committed to guarding the boundaries of his expertise very carefully, becomes more comfortable with his fellow team members, he will become freer in allocating tasks to others, who can often work under his supervision and learn by so doing.

An Overview of Interdisciplinary Knowledge

A major problem in preparing workers for interdisciplinary teamwork has been a lack of unifying concepts and principles that serve to tie the totality of knowledge together in a way that can be used. Modern thought is moving in the direction of development of a holistic theory that will serve to synthesize units into a whole and yet retain the integrity of the unit. As we better understand the nature of the invisible relationships between parts, this overall theory is emerging. The presently emphasized systems theory is an extremely useful tool in such organization, and as it is increasingly difficult to practice in this complex society without such knowledge, human service practitioners need to understand it. It is apparent that it can be validly applied not only to the physical universe but also to other aspects of life.

A detailed and comprehensive knowledge of the content of systems theory and of its utility as a set of organizing and understanding concepts in the nature of relationships between parts is no guarantee, however, that the possessor will be able to use it. The need is to teach potential team workers how to combine into a meaningful whole and yet retain their individual and group integrity. Of recent years, this problem of dealing with differences has been tackled in another area in human service, that of bringing people from various ethnic minorities into the mainstream of education, employment, and access to the benefits of the social system. The teaching techniques that have been employed successfully in this endeavor can be employed with equal effect in dealing with some of the problems presented by the minority groups created by specialization.

Initially, it is important to note that the basic philosophical stance underlying the meaning and importance of unique groups within the total society is in the process of change. Instead of the old concept of society as a melting pot in which all differences are integrated and blended into an amorphous whole, the uniqueness, strength, and importance of these differences are increasingly recognized. Society is now visualized as a complex of different but interlocking and collaborating groups. Certainly by the very nature of specialization, this concept must underlie teamwork. The clarity with which the differential strengths in specializations are perceived and utilized, particularly in role definition, is one of the basic determiners of success in team effort. The framework of collaboration and community within the team is built on recognition of difference, acceptance of pluralism, and realization of equality. That boundaries are not rigid and that there will be overlap is obvious, but the strong team can work in an arena in which constant negotiation can take place.

The great need of the student in intra- and intergroup relations is not only for knowledge of the groups involved but also for the ability to reach across these boundaries while at the same time respecting them. Just as one person cannot know all the details of differences among ethnic groups, so he cannot know all the details of work in other specialties. The individual needs, however, to develop a mind set that sensitizes him to the existence of differences and similarities; that enables him to deal with his ever-present tendency to perceive different groups as monolithic and to stereotype their representatives; that creates openness and nondefensiveness in communication; and that fosters realistic awareness of the social and cultural conditions, both within and without the specializations, that separate groups and their members rather than pull them together. He needs to have this mind set toward his own specialization, as well as others.

The importance of people-to-people learning in creating this mind set can hardly be overestimated. Human relationship is a medium through which both didactic and experiential learning are channelled. Involvement of representatives from various disciplines and emphasis on interaction among them is an essential part of teamwork education.

It is easy to become discouraged when working in the field of human relations, about which we are still largely illiterate. Norman Cousins once defined this state as a functional illiteracy, saying that in many instances, we know what we should do and how to do it, but we don't do it. Our insatiable curiosity, our physical and intellectual evolution have created conditions that have not only outstripped our ability to live with them but have sometimes actually been destructive to the totality of man. The fact that human life is an unending problem-solving process, inclusive of both the challenge and the opportunity of existence, was never more obvious than in the search for a process that will enable us to better deal with ourselves and our society. The team model of practice in human service represents one facet of this process, which with all of its problems and possibilities, merits careful consideration and testing.

Related Readings

Austin, Michael and Smith, Phillip: Statewide Career Planning in a Human Service Industry. Tallahassee, Fl.: University of Florida, 1973.
   Well-selected and presented collection of useful articles on planning, staffing, and delivering human services in a humanistic fashion (in spite of the title).
Blackey, Eileen: Group Leadership in Staff Training. Washington, D.C.: U.S. Dept. of Health, Education, and Welfare, 1956.
   Old but still valid combination of theory and application of theory in use of groups in learning.
Dyer, W.G. (Editor): New Dimensions in Group Training. New York: Van Nostrand, 1970.
   Usable collection of articles on current use of groups in training.
Havinghurst, Robert: Developmental Tasks and Education, second edition. New York: Longmans Green, 1952.
   Basic text relating learning ability and the various stages of life by one of the pioneers in the field.
Hunt, J. McV.: Intelligence and Experience. New York: Ronald, 1961.
   Good foundation reading in the relationship of experiences and cognitive ability.
Lewis, Robert et al.: A Systems Approach to Manpower Utilization and Training. Salt Lake City, Utah: Utah Division of Family Services, 1970.
   Task analysis approach to training and assignment of workers.
National Institute of Health: A Distillation of Principles on Research Utilization. Washington, D.C.: U.S. Dept. of Health, Education, and Welfare, 1973.
   Excellent analysis of research use, and a survey and evaluation of various current programs in the field.
Toffler, Alvin (Editor): Learning for Tomorrow—The Role of the Future in Education. New York: Random House, 1974.

Collection of articles by various authors representing a wide range of fields and disciplines, whose commonality is emphasis on trying to anticipate and prepare for the future.

Towle, Charlotte: The Learner in Education for the Professions. Chicago: University of Chicago Press, 1954.

Ageless and highly useful statement by one of the great educators.

Appendix A

invitation
to introspection

Introspection, the process of looking into oneself
with the objective of perceiving and beginning to
understand what exists and is happening there, is
never ending throughout life. Individuals vary
greatly in both motivation and ability to use this
process constructively. Yet it is an essential process for workers in the area of human service,
whose sensitivity to their own internal selves and
how they use these selves in their relationships
with other people is vital to the performance of
their jobs.

The most important aspect of any one person
is how he sees and feels about himself. This is the
foundation stone on which rests his ability to relate with others and cope with the demands of
living. The first small step toward understanding
what the self consists of is to examine oneself
knowledgeably—to introspect. The following
instruments have been constructed with the hope
that they will serve as tools in this essential process, to stimulate perceiving, thinking, feeling,
understanding, learning, and growing.

Instrument for Introspection, I

Principle: Only as we know ourselves as we are, not as we would like to be, can we be aware of what we are saying and doing to other people.

Question: Remembering that total self-awareness is impossible, what do I bring to interpersonal relationships? What do I communicate in myself as a person?

1. That generally I like and am comfortable with myself?

2. That sometimes I get discouraged and depressed about myself and life but I know that although there are bad times, there are always good times, too?

3. That I am pretty well satisfied with what I know, but I like new ideas and new experiences even though they sometimes make me uncomfortable?

4. That change does not come easy for me; I like things to stay the way they are?

5. That I get uncomfortable when people disagree with me and each other or talk about "unpleasant" things like fear, pain, anger, grief, guilt?

6. That I enjoy a good fight and don't carry grudges when I lose?

7. That I don't like to fight; that "my parents never fought in front of us children"?

8. That I worry about what will happen to me if I risk myself and would rather just let things slide?

9. That if someone attacks me, I fight back, say nothing, or put him on my list to get later?

10. That I enjoy challenge and change and "things happening"?

11. That, if necessary, I can stand alone?

12. That there is a part of myself I do not share with others?

13. That I am comfortable with, afraid of, or wary of people with power and authority?

14. That I generally anticipate (1) success or (2) failure as the probable outcome of an undertaking?

15. That I enjoy working with people?

Instrument for Introspection, II

Principle: An interpersonal relationship is a two-way street.

Question: What do I know (perceive clearly), think (have in mind), and feel (sense) about other people? How do I see them?

1. As generally good and to be trusted?

2. As generally bad and not to be trusted?

3. As generally a combination of both good and bad that I can accept and get along with?

4. As participants in a reciprocal relationship with me, knowing that if I attack, I am likely to be attacked in return, if I love, I am likely to be loved in return?

5. As acceptable as people, although disliking individual behavior, ideas, and feelings?

6. As not to be liked or trusted if they don't agree with me or have a life-style different from mine?

7. As taking advantage of me if I show weakness or indecision?

8. As making me uncomfortable when they don't conform to everyday social norms?

9. As evil when not socially responsible, according to my definition?

10. As capable of change?

11. As having a right to keep secrets about themselves?

12. As having the right to be themselves, to have a good life, and to make their own decisions?

13. As generally happier, smarter, luckier, and more socially skilled than I or as unhappier, more stupid, more inept, and less socially skilled than I?

14. As either people I can push around or people who will push me around?

15. As replications of significant other people in my own life?

a functional yardstick for team analysis

Each team, like each person, is unique and individual. We can, however, generalize to the extent of pinpointing vital areas in the life space of all teams which determine the success or failure of the teamwork. Each team must know the answers to the questions that arise in these areas, in light of their applicability to its unique self. Each must also be prepared to devote time and energy throughout its life span to keeping the answers up-to-date.

Purpose

1. What is the overall purpose of this team?
2. Who defines it?
3. Is there common understanding and agreement regarding its meaning among the various systems and individuals involved?
4. What is required to implement it?
5. What is required to change it?
6. Do the working goals grow naturally out of it?

A Functional Yardstick for Team Analysis

Composition and Structure

1. Who makes up this team?
2. How is this decided?
3. How are both original and additional members selected and involved?
4. How is membership changed?
5. What provision is made to enable the individual to become a team member?
6. How are the roles of the team members defined?
7. How is the effectiveness of both their uniqueness and their complementarity assessed?
8. How are roles changed?
9. Is there clear and common understanding of team composition and structure among the members?

Internal System

1. What is the underlying value system of this team?
2. How is it integrated with the value systems of the various team members?
3. What are the behavioral norms of this team?
4. How are they arrived at and integrated with the personal norms of the various team members?
5. How do they relate to institutional, community, and societal values and norms?
6. How are they enforced, evaluated, and changed?
7. What is the climate of this team?
8. How is it maintained and changed?
9. What are the relationships, personal and professional, among the team members?
10. Where does the power in this team lie?
11. How is it manifested and used?
12. How is it controlled and changed?
13. What are the pressures leading to conformity and groupthink in this team?
14. How are they managed?

Administration and Logistics

1. How is this team administered and managed?
2. What kind of leadership exists?

3. What is the relationship of leadership to administration?
4. How can leadership and administration be controlled and changed?
5. What are the essential logistics of this team's operation?
6. Who provides these supportive and maintenance services?
7. What provisions exist for their ongoing evaluation and change?

Internal Process

1. How does this team communicate within itself?
2. Is there a common language?
3. Is there provision for recognizing and working to clear clogged communication channels?
4. How does this team use discussion?
5. How does this team use conflict?
6. How does this team reach decisions?
7. How do the members of this team collaborate, accept, and implement decisions, both those which they support and those with which they disagree?
8. How does this team use authority?
9. How are individual and team tasks defined and implemented?
10. Does this team consciously use a problem-solving process?
11. How does it deal with breakdowns in this process?
12. How does this team arrange for necessary supervision of itself and its various members?
13. How does this team evaluate itself and its members?

Environment

1. What constitutes this team's environment?
2. What are the relationships involved here?
3. What are the channels of communication?
4. What is happening along the interfaces of the various systems within the environment?
5. What are the linkages between these various systems?
6. How are they used?
7. How are they evaluated and changed?
8. How is this team accountable to those who sanction its work: clients, institution, community, society?

A Functional Yardstick for Team Analysis

Self-actualization and Renewal

1. Is this team free and able to evaluate its own work?

2. What provisions does this team make for continuing education of itself and its members?

3. How does this team stimulate, recognize, and use innovation, creativity, and change?

4. Does this team possess the flexibility, in both its parts and its whole, to respond to crisis and change?

iNdEX